To Dr. Milton H. Erickson

Who Heals With Words

WATZLAWICK : Language of change

SOCIAL SCIENCE LIBRARY

Manor Road Building
Manor Road
Oxford OX1 3UQ
Tel: (2)71093 (enquiries and renewals)
http://www.ssl.ox.ac.uk

This is a NORMAL LOAN item.

We will email you a reminder before this item is due.

Please see http://www.ssl.ox.ac.uk/lending.html
for details on:

- loan policies; these are also displayed on the notice boards and in our library guide.

- how to check when your books are due back.

- how to renew your books, including information on the maximum number of renewals. Items may be renewed if not reserved by another reader. Items must be renewed before the library closes on the due date.

- level of fines; fines are charged on overdue books.

Please note that this item may be recalled during Term.

THE
LANGUAGE
OF
CHANGE

Elements of Therapeutic

Communication

PAUL WATZLAWICK

MENTAL RESEARCH INSTITUTE

PALO ALTO, CALIFORNIA

BASIC BOOKS, INC., PUBLISHERS

NEW YORK

ACKNOWLEDGMENTS

The cartoon on page 53 is reprinted with the permission of Magi Wechsler, the artist. The cartoon originally appeared in the *Neue Zürcher Zeitung* (NZZ) 49/70.

The advertisement on page 82 is reprinted courtesy of the Phillips-Van Heusen Corporation.

The cartoon on page 85 is reprinted by permission of the Newspaper Enterprise Association.

The excerpt on page 14 from "An Imperial Message" by Franz Kafka appears in *Parables and Paradoxes.* Copyright © 1946, 1947, 1948, 1953, 1954, 1958 by Schocken Books Inc. Copyright © renewed 1974 by Schocken Books Inc. Reprinted by permission.

The author gratefully acknowledges permission to reprint portions of the following material.

Max Frisch, *The Fire Raisers,* in *Three Plays,* trans. Michael Bullock (London: Methuen & Co., 1962). Reprinted by permission of Hill and Wang, Inc.

Hugo von Hofmannsthal, *The Difficult Man,* in *Plays and Libretti,* Bollingen Series, vol. 33, no. 3 (New York: Pantheon Books, 1963), pp. 712–713. Copyright © 1963 by Princeton University Press.

Jay Haley, *Uncommon Therapy: The Psychiatric Techniques of Milton H. Erickson, M.D.* (New York: W. W. Norton, 1973). Reprinted by permission of W. W. Norton, Inc. Copyright © 1963 by Jay Haley.

Milton Erickson, "The Use of Symptoms as an Integral Part of Hypnotherapy," *American Journal of Clinical Hypnosis* 8 (1965): 57–65. Reprinted by permission.

Milton Erickson and L. Rossi, "Varieties of Double Bind," *American Journal of Clinical Hypnosis* 17 (1975): 143–57. Reprinted by permission.

Library of Congress Cataloging in Publication Data

Watzlawick, Paul.
    The language of change.

    Bibliography: p. 161.
    Includes index.
    1. Psychotherapy. 2. Interpersonal communication. 3. Left and right (Psychology) I. Title.
RC480.5.W34   616.8'914   77-20416
ISBN: 0-465-03792-5

The Language of Change

BOOKS BY PAUL WATZLAWICK

An Anthology of Human Communication: Text and Tape

Pragmatics of Human Communication: A Study of Interactional Patterns, Pathologies and Paradoxes (with Janet H. Beavin and Don D. Jackson)

Change: Principles of Problem Formation and Problem Resolution (with John H. Weakland and Richard Fisch)

How Real Is Real?

The Interactional View: Studies at the Mental Research Institute, Palo Alto, 1965–74 (edited and with a commentary by Paul Watzlawick and John H. Weakland)

CONTENTS

PREFACE — ix

1. *Overview* — 3

2. *Our Two Languages* — 13

3. *Our Two Brains* — 19

4. *Experimental Evidence* — 28

5. *World Images* — 40

6. *Right-Hemispheric Language Patterns* — 48
   Condensations 49
   Figurative Language 56
   Pars pro toto 69
   Aphorisms 73
   Ambiguities, Puns, Allusions 78

7. *Blocking the Left Hemisphere* — 91
   Il est interdit d'interdire 99
   Symptom Prescriptions 101
   Symptom Displacements 106
   The Illusion of Alternatives 108
   Reframing 118

8. *Injunctive Language—Behavior Prescriptions* — 127

9. *Anything, Except THAT* — 138
   Speaking the Patient's "Language" 139
   Utilizing the Patient's Resistance 144
   Preempting 150

10. *Therapeutic Rituals*   154
11. *Conclusion*   158
     WORKS CITED   161
     INDEX   167

PREFACE

The thesis of this book is simple; its practical application is not. Monsieur Jourdain, the hero of Molière's comedy, *Le Bourgeois Gentilhomme*, wants to send his beloved a *billet-doux* and enlists the help of his preceptor for this task. The latter wants to know if it should be composed in verse or in prose. Monsieur Jourdain at first rejects both alternatives. Upon being informed that there is no third possibility, he cannot get over his astonishment that for forty years he should have been speaking prose without knowing it.

This book wants to show that very much the same holds true for the language of psychotherapy. Not only were the ancient rhetoricians fully aware of many of its essential properties, but many other characteristics have for a considerable time been the object of detailed studies in the most diverse areas of human experience—in childhood, language formation, fiction, wit, dream, ecstasy, intoxication, and delusion. But what thereby emerges from realms which on account of their sinister strangeness are ascribed to the unconscious, dark side of the soul is, in clinical dialogue, habitually translated into the supposedly therapeutic language of reason and consciousness. While upon reflection it should become obvious that this dark and often bizarre language holds the natural key to those areas alone in which therapeutic change can take place, this conclusion is rarely drawn. And like Monsieur Jourdain we are surprised when we finally discover that we have always known this language—albeit without knowing that we knew it.

So much for the thesis.

The practical, clinical use of this language is difficult and represents the subject matter of this book. It wants to be an introductory grammar, a language course, permitting the therapist to grasp the essence of this language and to use it for the benefit of his patients. This is easier said than done, and the book, therefore, can at best be a guide and not an instruction manual. As is known, the mere reading of a grammar does not in itself lead to the mastery of a language.

The reader who knows my book *How Real Is Real?* [115] will notice that the problems of reality perception and reality "construction," presented there in popular-scientific, anecdotal, and deliberately entertaining fashion, are treated here in the frame of psychotherapeutic language and technique, and that the two books thus complement each other. Furthermore, the present work is based on the principles of problem formation, problem resolution, and interpersonal communication described in our book *Change* [117].

The authors and colleagues whose work has contributed to the material presented here are too numerous to acknowledge individually. I have attempted to acquit myself of my indebtedness toward them by stating my sources as exactly and fully as possible. Quite naturally, however, I consider myself exclusively responsible for my use of these sources, as well as for the positions taken and any errors committed by me.

Preface

It is my pleasant duty to thank Mrs. Claire Bloom, Coordinator of Professional Activities at the Mental Research Institute, for her skillful help in the rapid production of the manuscript in its final form. Her work was made possible by a generous grant from Mr. William B. O'Boyle. His continued support of our Institute is gratefully acknowledged.

P. W.

The Language of Change

1

Overview

ONE CAN free children from warts by "purchasing" them. In practice this is achieved by giving the child a coin for, and thus laying a claim to, his wart. As a rule the child then asks—amused or bewildered—how he is supposed to let go of the wart, whereupon one answers nonchalantly that he should not worry about that—the wart will come off all by itself.

Although the effectiveness of all kinds of magical and superstitious treatments of warts has been known since time immemorial, there does not exist a scientifically satisfactory explanation of these treatments; especially not for the procedure just mentioned. What happens is really quite extraordinary: A totally absurd, symbolic interaction leads to a concrete result; that is, the blood vessels leading into this virally produced tissue begin to constrict, and the wart eventually atrophies as a result of anoxia. This, however, means that the use of a specific interpersonal communication leads not merely to a change of the mood, the views, or the feelings of its recipient, as it can be observed on an everyday basis, but to a *physical* change that cannot "normally" be effected deliberately.

On the other hand, it is only too well known that our emotions can make us physically sick, that we can hypnotize ourselves into illness, as it were, without—like Monsieur Jourdain—knowing that we have always mastered this pathogenic "prose" in our communications with ourselves. But this means no more nor less that, according to the principle *similia similibus curantur*, it must be possible to use this same language in the service of healing.

Or to express the same assumption in a somewhat different way: There exist countless examples of the life-threatening or life-saving effect of emotions, fantasies, and especially of the influence that humans can have on their fellow humans. We need not draw upon such exotic instances as the concrete results of dramatic curses, the phenomenon of voodoo-death, or the often quite incredible successes of spiritual healers in order to comprehend that there has to exist a language which produces these effects. And it then makes sense to assume that this language can be studied and learned at least to a certain degree.*

The acquisition and use of this language thus becomes the obvious and urgent concern of a psychotherapeutic approach which places emphasis on concrete, technical skills and which is skeptical of the esoteric effusions of many a modern school. I would even go so far as to claim that, when using this language, the question as to what particular school of thought a therapist subscribes to becomes quite unimportant, and that probably most of those surprising and unexpected improvements—for which the particular theory does not provide a satisfactory explanation and

---

* To avoid misunderstandings, it should be emphasized that I am not referring to the *intraorganismic* (e.g., hormonal, neurological, metabolic) communications—although their study, too, is of the greatest scientific interest and relevance—but to the question of how these processes can be initiated, controlled, and reinforced through communication from the *outside*.

which, therefore, are not "supposed" to take place—can be traced back to the unintentional and fortuitous use of the patterns of communication referred to above.

The fact that communication is a *conditio sine qua non* of human existence has been known for a very long time. In Fra Salimbene of Parma's chronicle of the life of Frederick II there is a reference to an experiment instituted by the emperor himself and intended to discover man's primal language. For this purpose, he had several newly born infants raised by nurses who had strict orders to attend to all their needs but to refrain from the use of language in their presence. By producing this linguistic vacuum, the emperor hoped to establish whether the children would spontaneously begin to speak Hebrew, Greek, or Latin. Unfortunately for Frederick—let alone the babies—the result of the experiment remained inconclusive; in spite of the excellence of its research design it was, in Salimbene's words, "to no avail, for the little ones all died" [96]. Seven centuries later René Spitz, in his studies on marasmus and hospitalism [108], provided the modern explanation for the disastrous result of the emperor's excursion into psycholinguistics.*

* In light of these facts, we have to dismiss as unbelievable the story of the mysterious Kaspar Hauser, who appeared in Nuremberg in May 1828 with an anonymous letter of recommendation to the authorities but was unable to shed any light on his life and origin, except to claim that he was 16 years old and had always been kept completely alone in a dark cubicle. He soon became the object of many romantic theories (and of a recent film), and the mystery surrounding him was perpetuated when, on 14 December 1833, he returned home with several stab wounds, allegedly inflicted by unknown assailants, and died a few days later.

In the environment that he described, Kaspar Hauser would never have had a chance to survive, let alone to develop into an adolescent. Almost the exact opposite appears to have taken place in an unusual example of language development reported by the linguist Jespersen. It suggests that where the preconditions of communication exist, language develops almost like a primitive force. Jespersen reported the case of a girl, born at the beginning of the last century on a farm in northern Iceland, who

began early to converse with her twin brother in a language that was entirely unintelligible to their surroundings. Her parents were disquieted, and therefore resolved to send away the brother, who died soon afterwards. They now tried to teach the girl Icelandic, but soon (too soon, evidently!) came to the conclusion that she could not

5

That language is a powerful determinant of moods, views, behavior and especially of decisions was, of course, known at least 1500 years before Frederick II. Suffice it to think of the high esteem in which already the pre-Socratic philosophers held rhetoric and its closely related discipline, sophistry. It is interesting to note that rhetoric, as a consistent doctrine,* was in a very real sense the precursor of modern communications research in that it was related not to a specific subject area or topic, but was a discipline *in itself*—just as the study of the pragmatics of communication [116] deals with communication as a phenomenon

---

learn it, and then they were foolish enough to learn *her* language, as did also her brothers and sisters and even some of their friends. In order that she might be confirmed, her elder brother translated the catechism and acted as interpreter between the parson and the girl. She is described as intelligent—she even composed poetry in her own language—but shy and distrustful. [64]

A similar, very recent example is the case of the identical, six year old twins Grace and Virginia Kennedy. Since they had had seizures shortly after birth and had subsequently failed to show normal language development, they were considered severely retarded. Their case quickly gained attention in July 1977, when a speech therapist at the Children's Hospital in San Diego discovered that the girls not only understood English and German (the language in which their grandmother talked to them), although they did not *speak* either, but had learned sign language as a result of their therapy, and, in addition, fluently conversed with each other in a private language of their own creation.—Although I know of no systematic studies, the emergence of this kind of language (at least temporarily) has been reported by several parents of twins, and may be a far more common phenomenon than one might assume.

* It may be useful to list here—following Kopperschmidt—the different meanings of the term. The second of these definitions applies here, while the third obviously means the communicational ability to which this book wants to contribute:

1. "Rhetoric" in its meaning of *theory* or *doctrine of speaking* (e.g., "Modern rhetoric is still in the phase of basic research"). In this sense "rhetoric" means the study (in research as well as teaching) of rhetorical speech, its structure, function, system, manifestations, applications, history, etc.
2. "Rhetoric" in its meaning of a general *art of speaking* (e.g., "The power of rhetoric has often been abused"). In this sense it means a system of rules and techniques whose application ensures an optimal persuasive effect.
3. "Rhetoric" in its meaning of an *individual verbal skill* (e.g., "His rhetoric is excellent"). In this sense it means the—conscious or unconscious—mastery of the above-mentioned rules and techniques in their various forms of language usage by a verbalizing individual. [72, p. 13]

in its own right rather than with the content and the meaning of messages in a specific context or subject area. But in those days, just as occasionally also today, this very lack of specific content was found disturbing; and the impossibility of conceptually assigning rhetoric to a specific, superordinate discipline, as well as its claim that the skilled rhetorician would be victorious in any contest with any expert, had the result of making the art of persuasion even more suspect and contemptible. This may be one of the main reasons why Socrates, among others, was against the rhetoricians and the sophists. Aristotle, on the other hand, was in favor of rhetoric and conceived of it as—to state it in modern terms—a form of communication between a man of high standing, prestige, and trustworthiness and the recipient of his messages, whose mind and outlooks are thereby changed. But while Aristotle's idea of rhetoric is quite unobjectionable in theory, he seems to have been less than squeamish about it in actual practice, for especially in his *Rhetorica ad Alexandrum* * [Rhetoric for Alexander] there are passages of surprising callousness and cynicism.

But of all the thinkers of that distant era it is Antiphon of Athens (480–411 B.C.) who appears to have come closest to the modern concept of therapeutic communication. Little is known about him and his life; it is not even certain if Antiphon, the sophist, and Antiphon, the healer, were one and the same person. But there exists fragmentary information which indicates that Antiphon was the inventor of an "art of solace" and apparently believed that it would eventually be possible to cast the phenomena of persuasion and other verbal influence into a consistent theoretical framework. To the extent that his main endeavor appears to have been the discovery and therapeutic appli-

---

* A work attributed by some scholars not to Aristotle but to Anaximenes of Lampsacus.

cation of the hidden rules of verbal interaction, it does not seem too far-fetched to consider him the precursor of modern pragmatics. To this end, Antiphon would first encourage the patient to talk about his suffering and would then help him by means of a rhetoric which utilized both style and content of the patient's utterances—a procedure which in a very modern sense amounted to a *reframing* of that which the sufferer considered "real" or "true," and thereby changed his pain-producing world image.

Plutarch writes of Antiphon:

While he was still engaged in poetry he invented an art of liberation from pain, just as for those who are sick there is a treatment by physicians. In Corinth he was given a house beside the *Agora* and put up a sign to the effect that he was able to heal by words those who were sick. [88]

In a similar vein, Plato lets his Gorgias boast of the power of rhetoric:

On several occasions I have been with my brother Herodicus or some other physician to see one of his patients, who would not allow the physician to give him medicine, or apply the knife or hot iron to him; and I have persuaded him to do for me what he would not do for the physician just by the use of rhetoric. [85]

Plato himself is considered the father of *catharsis*, the art of the purification of the soul. There is no doubt that already he, as well as the Hippocratic physicians, aimed at the abreaction of emotions through verbal means. By the third century B.C. this principle was adopted especially by the stoics and was made the main tenet of their view that all troubles of the soul and their concomitant obfuscations of the eternal light of reason were to be sought in the irrational effects of feelings.

In the first century A.D. Quintilian, in his *Institutio Oratoria*

Overview

[The Training of an Orator], contributes the important (and, again, very modern-sounding) concept of *somatic rhetoric*. In it he enumerates and describes the various optical and acoustic "styles" that can be used by an orator, detailed knowledge of which will enhance his persuasive powers. During the last twenty-five years, many of Quintilian's concepts have been rediscovered, so to speak, and described under such terms as *kinesics, body language, paralinguistic phenomena*, and, generally, *non-verbal communication*. In common with the rhetoricians, Quintilian believed that the ability to convince the interlocutor was of decisive importance. Of course, in order to be persuasive, somatic rhetoric has to be accompanied by the appropriate use of words; that is, by the right *pronuntiatio* (delivery):

If delivery can count for so much in themes which we know to be fictitious and devoid of reality, as to arouse our anger, our tears or our anxiety, how much greater must its effect be when we actually believe what we hear? For my own part I would not hesitate to assert that a mediocre speech supported by all the power of delivery will be more impressive than the best speech unaccompanied by such power. [92]

Not surprisingly, rhetoric was not only criticized for its "emptiness"—that is, for the fact, already mentioned in the foregoing, that rhetoric does not belong to a particular discipline and, indeed, claims to be somewhat of a metadiscipline—but an even more serious accusation was leveled against it: that it could serve the good as well as the evil, truth as well as falsehood. This, too, is mentioned in Plato's *Gorgias:*

And yet, Socrates, rhetoric should be used like any other competitive art—the rhetorician ought not to abuse his strength any more than a pugilist or pancratiast or other master of fence;—because he has powers which are more than a match either for friend or enemy, he ought not therefore to strike, stab, or slay his friends. Suppose a man to have been trained in the palestra and to be a skilful boxer,—he in the fulness of his strength goes and strikes his father or mother or one of his familiars or friends; but that is no reason why the trainers or fencing-masters should be held in detestation or banished from the city;—surely not. For they taught their art for a good purpose, to be used against enemies and evil-doers, in self-defense not in aggression, and others have perverted their instructions, and turned to a bad use their own strength and skill. But not on this account are the teachers bad, neither is the art in fault, or bad in itself; I should rather say that those who make a bad use of the art are to blame. And the same argument holds good of rhetoric. [85]

Twenty-five hundred years have not changed this problem in the least. What Plato says concerning rhetoric is just as true for modern communications research, for the psychotherapeutic conclusions that can be drawn from it, and therefore also for this book. All that heals can also be abused; just as, conversely, a poison can also cure. But especially today *any* form of influence, in particular anything that can be labeled as manipulation, is attacked and condemned as being unethical. These attacks are not merely directed at the abuses of manipulation—which, needless to say, are always possible—but to manipulation as such. Their origin seems to be the blind, utopian belief that human coexistence is either possible without any mutual influence whatsoever, or at least in the apparently so ideal sense of Fritz Perls' "Gestalt Prayer": "You do your thing and I do my thing. . . ." Out of this basic premise it is then possible to develop therapies that all but drip with pseudosincerity and whose common denominator is the contention that they are free from all manipulation.* Since I

* Although this cult of sincerity, spontaneity, and candor has now begun to spread also to Europe, it appears to be a primarily North American phenomenon. Professor Evans, a scholar of English literature who came to Stanford University from his native England, gives an excellent summary of the different styles of communication in Europe and in the United States:

The belief that everything is, or should be, apprehensible to the outside world thus seems to have led to the establishment of sincerity as the dominant norm governing

Overview

have presented some of the practical consequences of this utopia elsewhere [117, pp. 47–61; 115, pp. 22–25], I shall merely summarize here: One cannot *not* influence. It is, therefore, absurd to ask how influence and manipulation can be avoided, and we are left with the inescapable responsibility of deciding for ourselves how this basic law of human communication may be obeyed in the most humane, ethical, and effective manner.

Those who find these facts repugnant and wish to turn away from them in hostility or disappointment would do well to consider what even so uncompromising an opponent of the modern "consciousness industry"* as Enzensberger has to say about this dilemma:

Let us . . . draw the line between intellectual integrity and defeatism. To opt out of the mind industry, to refuse any dealings with it may well turn out to be a reactionary course. There is no hermitage left for those

---

personal relationships in this country, at least as Europeans perceive it. Sincerity, after all, is simply a form of human transparency. A sincere person is an individual-without-the-walls, a self that allows you to see into its interior. In the presence of such a person, one feels assured, nothing is being concealed, nothing is being held in reserve or masked by a veil of irony, understatement, or wit—the three favorite modes of European discourse.

One obvious manifestation of this reverence for candor is the cult of informality in American dress and American speech—the almost immediate use of first names, for instance, rather than the more distant impersonal modes of address. For first names, like casual clothes, suggest ease, openness, the frankness of familiarity, whereas formality implies reserve and consequently a certain degree of concealment. Another less obvious manifestation of the same impulse may be a phenomenon that puzzled me for a long time after my arrival in this country, namely the fact that puns, which are so prized in Great Britain, are generally greeted by Americans with groans of disapproval. The reason, I have come to suspect, is that any form of *double-entendre* reminds us that words as well as people are capable of having hidden meanings, that the very language we use to communicate with each other is not always completely "sincere."

And Evans speculates that "anything smacking of overt dissimulation is bound to seem particularly threatening to an illusionistic society that insists on pretending to be real." [32]

* By this term, Enzensberger means the subtle but powerful ways in which the mass media, the politicians, the societal effects of science, and the stultification produced by the advertising industry influence and shape the opinions of the citizens.

11

whose job it is to speak out and to seek innovation. Retreat from the media will not even save the individual's precious soul from corruption. *It might be a better idea to enter the dangerous game, to take and calculate our risks.* [24; italics mine]

Yet another utopia—the twin sister of the cult of sincerity—needs to be mentioned to chart the position of this book: Like a subterranean stream, from the ancient philosophers to the present day, surfacing again and again in all its majestic power of conviction, there runs the belief that reason is the highest faculty and that with its help man can grasp the real reality as it objectively exists "out there." More will have to be said in the pages of this book about the persistence of this utopia in modern psychiatry, where the unquestioned belief in an objective reality, whose properties are accessible to normal people, determines the concepts of sanity and madness. It shall be argued that this view is untenable and that we can only talk about interpretations of reality, of *world images*, but not about reality *itself*.

Our Two Languages

> Let us learn to dream, gentlemen, and then
> perhaps we shall learn the truth.
> —August Kekulé, 1865

IF WE LOOK over the preceding pages, we find that, by and large, their content is in keeping with what one would expect from a professional work: a preface, an introduction to the subject matter, the usual historical references, some personal views of the author, and so forth. Similarly, the form of presentation—the way these pages try to enter into communication with the reader—also adheres to the norm: the language is explanatory; it conveys information (about whose value one may have very different opinions); it is cerebral, intellectual, and, apart from the author's personal views, fairly objective.

Let us suppose, however, that—rather incongruously—I had begun this book with a quotation from Kafka's parable, *An Imperial Message.* From his deathbed, the Emperor has sent a message to you, the humble subject, the insignificant shadow:

The messenger immediately sets out on his journey; a powerful, an indefatigable man; now pushing with his right arm, now with his left, he cleaves a way for himself through the throng; if he encounters resistance he points to his breast, where the symbol of the sun glitters; the way, too, is made easier for him than it would be for any other man. But the multitudes are so vast; their numbers have no end. If he could reach the open fields how fast he would fly, and soon doubtless you would hear the welcome hammering of his fists on your door. But instead how vainly does he wear out his strength; still he is only making his way through the chambers of the innermost palace; never will he get to the end of them; and if he succeeded in that nothing would be gained; he must fight his way next down the stair; and if he succeeded in that nothing would be gained; the courts would still have to be crossed; and after the courts the second outer palace; and once more stairs and courts; and once more another palace; and so on for thousands of years; and if at last he should burst through the outermost gate—but never, never can that happen—the imperial capital would lie before him, the center of the world, crammed to bursting with its own refuse. Nobody could fight his way through here, least of all one with a message from a dead man.—But you sit at your window when evening falls and dream it to yourself. [66]

This, too, is language, but a language that influences us very differently, that resonates on other levels of our experience. It would be very difficult to explain why and how we are influenced by this language, how the palace's nightmarish vastness, teeming with humanity to the point of claustrophobia, becomes our own immediate experience, how it happens that suddenly it is we who are sitting by the window, longing for the message that would transfigure our lives, but will never arrive. It would indeed be futile to endeavor a translation from this into our everyday language, which at best can dissect images but not evoke them.

There are thus two languages involved. The one, in which for instance this sentence itself is expressed, is objective, definitional, cerebral, logical, analytic; it is the language of reason, of science, explanation, and interpretation, and therefore the language of most schools of psychotherapy. The other, in which the preceding example is expressed, is much more difficult to define—precisely because it is not the language of definition. We might call it the language of imagery, of metaphor, of *pars pro toto*, perhaps of symbols, but certainly of synthesis and totality, and not of analytical dissection.

The psychology of thinking, it will be remembered, draws a similar distinction between directed and undirected thoughts. The former follows the laws of linguistic logic; that is, of grammar, syntax and semantics. Undirected thinking is the stuff dreams, fantasies, and other experiences of our inner world are made of. It lacks direction only by comparison to directed thinking, for it does have its own "illogical" rules and regularities which express themselves in jokes, word games, puns, innuendos, and condensations.

In linguistics and in communication research we find an almost identical polarity; namely, that between the digital and analogic modalities. They offer two different ways of expressing a given meaning. In the digital mode it is communicated by a sign whose relation to the intended meaning is a purely conventional and thus quite arbitrary one, albeit one which must of necessity be shared by all its users if communication is to take place. A simple example would be any word on this page. Between it and its meaning there is no immediate, self-explanatory or directly understandable connection, but merely the tacit convention that this string of symbols (or, in the case of spoken language, of sounds) shall have that specific meaning in English. For this form of representation the term *digital* was taken over from mathematics. The other possibility is the use of a sign which does have some immediately obvious relation to the thing it signifies (the *significatum*) in that it represents a likeness or analogy; hence the term *analogic*. Examples would be maps and their relation to the territory they represent (except, of course, the geographical names printed on them), images and pictorial signs of all kinds (although continued use may eventually digitalize them, as is the case with most signs in Chinese writing), true symbols (and not only allegories) as they emerge in dreams, onomatopoetic words (such as *crash, hiss, bang*), *pars-pro-toto* representations (in which certain parts stand for the whole), and so forth.

The fact that there exist these two "languages" very strongly suggests that they must be representative of two very different *world images*, for it is known that a language does not so much *reflect* reality as *create* it.* And indeed, it can be shown how this polarity runs through the millennia of human thought, through philosophy, psychology, the arts, religion, and even the supposedly objective natural sciences—much more frequently as a schism than as harmonious complementarity. It may be useful to recall, for instance, C. G. Jung's typology which juxtaposes thought with feeling and perception with intuition, and thus expresses two diametrically different ways of grasping reality: a logical, methodic, and step-wise approach which at times may not see the forest for the trees; and the other, a global, holistic perception of totalities, of *Gestalten*, which occasionally may find it very difficult to cope with detail—and thus be unable to see the trees for the forest. To integrate these two antagonistic modalities appears to be the hallmark of genius: "The solution I already know," Gauss is supposed to have said on a certain occasion, "what now remains to be done is to find the way by which I have arrived at it." And Darboux, in his biography of another famous mathematician, Henri Poincaré, mentions that "when

---

* This is easier said than accepted. "For thousands of years," remarks Schneider,

it has been the philosophers' conviction, it is the unquestioned assumption of all children, and seems to be indelibly imprinted in the minds of most adults that words exactly represent reality, that sentences must have a meaning and that our environment *is* the way it is *called* in our mother tongue. Hence the indignation of the South-Tyrolian about the Italians, because they call a horse "cavallo": "We call it 'Pferd' and it *is* a Pferd." [98, pp. 193–94]

one asked him to solve a difficulty the reply came like an arrow."
[19] These statements contain two important facts in a nutshell:
First, the almost unbelievable ability of the mathematical genius
to anticipate, "somehow" and immediately, the result of even
very complicated problems, so that the real problem lies in the
methodic proof of the correctness of his *a priori* result*; and second, that—as even we laymen can appreciate—a schism runs
through the analytical and the intuitive currents of the philosophy and the epistemology of mathematics. A similar chasm separates orthodoxy from mysticism in most universal religions: On
the one side we find the conviction that the word of God is accessible to the individual only through the mediation of the priests
and the holy scriptures; on the other, there stand the *enfants ter-
ribles* of orthodoxy, the mystics, in their uncompromising rejection of liturgy and the dogmatic tenets of revelation, and their insistence on beholding the Godhead face to face.

All this and much more has been known, at least empirically,
for a long time. In the course of the last few decades, however,
unexpected scientific evidence for this duality of the mind has
been supplied by modern brain research. It is one of those rare
instances in which the exact sciences lead to an objective understanding of not only isolated psychological functions (like perception, memory, and so on), torn out of their natural interplay with
all the others, but of a phenomenon which—as we have seen—
runs across many areas of human experience and activity. It
would appear that for the first time we now hold the key to an objective understanding of those functional mental mechanisms
and disturbances (for example, repression, depersonalization, de-

---

* An interesting example from the field of engineering is the Schwandbach bridge in
the Swiss canton of Bern, completed in 1933. Its roadway forms a horizontal curve, and
this enormously complicated the necessary computations (a quarter of a century before
the advent of the computer!). The genius of its designer, Robert Maillart, is evidenced by
the fact that the computations, showing the correctness of his specifications, were not
completed until *after* the bridge was already built and opened to traffic.

17

lusion, and others), for whose explanation we have for so long had to rely on nebulous, speculative hypotheses. But new light is thereby also shed on those phenomena which scientists (or, for that matter, also artists and inventors) experience as the sudden, flashlike resolution of a problem with which they may have grappled for an excruciatingly long time. Kekulé's "dream" of the benzene ring* comes to mind here, as do the many examples which Koestler has collected in his *Act of Creation* [71] or that Kuhn has included in his now classic treatise on the structure of scientific revolutions [73].

* In his often-quoted biographical account he described this experience as follows:

I was sitting writing at my textbook, but the work did not progress; my thoughts were elsewhere. I turned my chair to the fire, and dozed. Again the atoms were gamboling before my eyes. This time the smaller groups kept modestly in the background. My mental eye, rendered more acute by repeated visions of this kind, could now distinguish larger structures of manifold conformations; long rows, sometimes more closely fitted together; all twisting and turning in snake-like motion. But look! What was that? One of the snakes had seized hold of its own tail, and the form whirled mockingly before my eyes. As if by a flash of lightning I woke; . . . I spent the rest of the night working out the consequences of the hypothesis. Let us learn to dream, gentlemen, and then perhaps we shall learn the truth. [67]

The great inventor Nikola Tesla seems to have possessed not only this ability to grasp the image of a complex solution in a flash of sudden inspiration. He was capable of sustaining these periods of imagery and to test his mental constructs as if they were real machines:

. . . It was not necessary for him to construct models of copper and iron: in his mental workshop he constructed them in a wide variety. A constant stream of ideas was continuously rushing through his mind. . . .
The mental constructs were built with meticulous care as concerned size, strength, design and material; and they were tested mentally, he maintained, by having them run for weeks, after which time he would examine them thoroughly for signs of wear. Here was a most unusual mind being utilized in a most unusual way. If he at any time built a "mental machine," his memory ever afterward retained all of the details, even to the finest dimensions. [82, pp. 51-52]

His ability to visualize must indeed have been prodigal:

Tesla could project before his eyes a picture, complete in every detail, of every part of the machine. These pictures were more vivid than any blueprint and he remembered exact dimensions which he had calculated mentally for each item. He did not have to test parts through partial assembly. He knew they would fit. [82, p. 55]

3

Our Two Brains

THERE USUALLY EXISTS a family myth about twins, especially monozygotic ones: One of them is the "intellectual," the other the "artist."

On the other hand, it is no myth that we all carry with us such a pair of twins inside our skull: our two hemispheres which, far from being a seemingly unnecessary duplication, are—as we now know—two separate brains with very different functions.

Somewhat more concretely than Goethe, who regretfully concluded that two souls dwell in our bosom, the British physician and anatomist Wigan discovered as early as 1844 that two minds do reside in our heads:

I believe myself then able to prove—1. That each cerebrum is a distinct and perfect whole as an organ of thought. 2. That a separate and distinct process of thinking or ratiocination may be carried on in each cerebrum simultaneously. [120, p. 26]

Wigan's basis for this view was anatomical evidence from *post mortem* examinations, one of which he describes as follows:

One hemisphere was entirely gone—that was evident to my senses; the patient, a man of about 50 years of age, had conversed rationally and even written verses within a few days of his death. [120, p. 40]

And he refers to a similar, typical case, seen by one of his colleagues:

Dr. Conolly mentions the case of a gentleman who had so serious a disease that it spread through the orbit into the cerebrum, and by very slow degrees destroyed his life. . . . On examining the skull, one brain was entirely destroyed—gone, annihilated—and in its place (in the narrator's emphatic language) "a yawning chasm." All of his mental faculties were quite perfect and his mind was clear and undisturbed to within a few hours of his death. [120, p. 41]

Wigan is thus one of the fathers of modern brain research. His acumen was all the more remarkable because he had to draw his conclusions exclusively from the clinical pictures of severest brain damage and, of course, he lacked the evidence, now available to researchers, of the psychological and behavioral consequences of cerebral *commissurotomy*. By this term is meant the separation of the two halves of the brain by means of the surgical dissection of their largest area of contact, the *corpus callosum*.*
Similar to Wigan's observations with his brain-damaged subjects, here, too—in spite of the severity of the intervention—no significant alterations in the patients' behavior can be observed upon superficial examination. Only detailed studies reveal changes in their mental functioning; these studies, however, permit fundamental conclusions to be drawn about the respective functions of the two hemispheres. Since these conclusions are of immedi-

* The most frequent reason for this intervention is the necessity to prevent the spreading of electric disrhythmias from one hemisphere into the other in those patients whose epileptic seizures respond poorly or not at all to the usual treatment by medication.

Our Two Brains

ate relevance to the subject matter of this book, I shall attempt to summarize them here.

In the typical right-handed person,* the *left* hemisphere is the dominant one, and its main function appears to be the translation of perceptions into logical, semantic, and phonetic representations of reality, and the communication with the outside world on the basis of this logical-analytical coding of the surrounding world. It is, therefore, competent for all that has to do with language (that is, grammar, syntax, semantics), with thinking, and thus also with reading, writing, counting, computing, and, generally, digital communication. Consequently, in the literature it is often referred to as the *verbal*, or major, hemisphere. In the Rorschach test, the left hemisphere presumably supplies the detail responses. In the psychoanalytic framework, the functions of the left hemisphere are virtually synonymous with the concept of secondary processes. It is also the origin of conscious innervations and thus gives dominance to the right (that is, contralateral) hand, thereby degrading the left hand to the role of a mere

---

* The simplistic assumption that in the left-handed person the dominance relation of the hemispheres is probably reversed is now being challenged. While it was generally assumed that during the first two years of life the two hemispheres develop equally and then begin to differentiate as language is acquired, research on the structure and function of infant brains [114] shows that the left half of the brain is predisposed for language development at least from birth, and that, therefore, left-handedness may not simply be the cause or the result of brain differentiation after birth. Detailed experiments, carried out by Dewson at Stanford University, have pushed the appearance of cerebral asymmetry even much further back into evolution. He has been able to show that in a rudimentary way it already exists in the monkey, a notoriously preverbal animal; and in a recent presentation, he summarizes his findings as follows:

> For now . . . we are able to say that mammalian left-brain, right-brain asymmetry does not exist solely for language, though it may in fact be a necessary condition. Monkeys were around, and were evolving, for scores of millions of years before us, and they still do not have language. Indeed, their natural behavior does not, so far, reveal to us either the presence, or even the need, for hemispheric asymmetry, and it is only by eliciting from them, in the laboratory, an artifical behavior that we have detected clues to the development of our brain organization. By short-circuiting the evolutionary process, we can see that inside every monkey sits a little bit of man. [20]

handyman. As already mentioned, as a result of its specialization the left hemisphere runs the danger of not seeing the forest for the trees. Lesions of the left hemisphere will lead to handicaps related to speech, writing, counting, computing, and reasoning. The strangest complications can be observed; for instance, one patient with total left hemispherectomy (surgical removal of the hemisphere) could *sing* the words of a song, but was unable to use any of these words singly—that is, outside the context (the *Gestalt*) of the song [106, p. 124]

The function of the *right* hemisphere is very different: It is highly specialized in the holistic grasping of complex relationships, patterns, configurations, and structures. Most of the clinical and experimental evidence seems to suggest that this ability must be somehow akin to the technique of holography,* for the right hemisphere not only masters the perception and recognition of a *Gestalt* from the most diverse angles and consequent relative distortions (a natural ability of the brain which still presents great problems for computer simulation), but that it may manage to perceive and recognize the totality from a very small portion of the latter. This enables us, for instance, to recognize a person although we may see only a tiny part of his face, very much as a musician may identify a concert or a symphony on the basis of one single bar or even just one chord. This ability of the right hemisphere seems to be based on the *pars-pro-toto* principle, that is, the immediate recognition of a totality on the basis of *one* essential detail.† In this connection, it is useful to emphasize the well-known fact that olfactory perceptions are particularly

---

* A photographic technique using coherent light (laser beams) rather than lenses. The negative (hologram) thus obtained permits an optical reconstruction of the photographed object in space (i.e., in three dimensions). Perhaps the most remarkable feature of this technique is that the *whole* image can be reconstructed from any *part* of the hologram.

† This should not be confused with the gradual and mosaic aggregation of many single details by the left hemisphere.

conducive to the mental reconstruction and reexperiencing of past events in their totality. The smell of blood may instantaneously reactivate the memory and the horror of a combat situation that has remained repressed for decades; the scent of jasmine or honeysuckle may lead back into the splendor of a Mediterranean landscape or the sweetness of a very early, timid love experience.

Similarly, any good caricature, conveying with the utmost economy of lines a complex totality, is proof for this *pars-pro-toto* perception and evocation of reality by the right half of the brain. Conversely, it is notoriously difficult to describe a face clearly and unambiguously in the analytical language of the left hemisphere [42, p. 574].*

In criminal investigations, where the exact description of faces by witnesses is of vital importance, this inability of left-hemispheric language to express the essential *Gestalt* of a face is circumvented by means of an identification kit, composed of many different facial elements, out of which the witness can construct the face as he remembers it, without having to rely on language.

What is of particular importance, however, is the strong likelihood that the right hemisphere is competent for the construction of logical classes and therefore for the formation of concepts— two abilities without which our perception of reality would be a kaleidoscopic chaos. This is to say that when we use concepts (like "triangle" and "table," for instance), we mean abstractions

---

* Cf. also Levy on this subject:

Faces, after all, are strongly resistant to analytic description. We do not recognize people by noting that, "This person has dark hair, blue eyes, freckles, and glasses and that therefore it must be Mary." We do so by an almost instantaneous perception of the essential *Gestalt*. Possibly the language-competent left hemisphere must rely on the inductive method and is in large part lacking any ability to visualize stimuli which are resistant to verbal description. [76]

which do not exist *as such*. Rather, we mean their quintessence (the logical *class*), so to speak, of all existing or imaginable triangles,* tables, and so forth. Without this ability to order the chaotic complexity of the world into logical classes, both human and animal existence would be impossible.

In psychoanalytic terminology the functions of the right hemisphere are virtually identical with the concept of the primary processes. Its associations are nonlinear and shed new light on the nature of free associations. As Freud postulated for the Id, so the right half of our brain is "timeless" both in a positive as well as a negative sense; that is, its contents appear to be much more resistant to time, but its orientation in time and its perceptions of temporal sequences are much less differentiated than those of the left half.

Its language is archaic and underdeveloped—so much so that the right hemisphere is often referred to in the literature as the "silent one." It lacks the prepositions and virtually all the other elements of (left-hemispheric) grammar, syntax, and semantics. Its concepts are ambiguous (very similar to what Freud called the "antithetical sense of primal words"). It tends to draw illogical conclusions based on clang associations and confusions of literal and metaphorical meanings, to use condensations, composite words, ambiguities, puns, and other word games—that is, language forms which in psychopathology are mostly considered to be the manifestations of schizophrenia. In the Rorschach test, it probably supplies the whole response.

The right hemisphere's archaic language is matched by a primitive arithmetic. Its upper limit is the addition of two single-digit

---

* We have it from Pierce:

As Berkeley points out, the abstract idea of a (or the ideal) triangle must at once be "neither oblique, rectangle, equilateral, equicrural nor scaleron, but all and none of these at once." [84]

numbers and thus remains below 20 [107, p. 731]; but, on the other hand, it is capable of very precise, immediate perceptions of quantity. Primitive herdsmen, for instance, whose ability to count is limited to the three numerals, *one, two*, and *many*, notice immediately if and which animals may be missing, even if the herd is very large.

The right hemisphere is also considerably better equipped than the left in the cognitive abilities necessary for the perception of complex spatial configurations; and it possesses a more or less consolidated *world image*—a fact that will occupy us again when we turn to examining the therapeutic implications of these research results. It is the image that dominates here, the analogy, and therefore also the recall of memories and of the moods and sensations that originally went with them. Many years ago the philosopher Jaspers had already remarked:

It is possible to "think," rather than in verbal concepts, in images, shapes, myths, gods, in landscapes, colors, natural phenomena, in terms of action and performance. All primitive world images evolve in this way, verbal language refers to it.

However, for Jaspers this mode of thinking is only a transition to verbal language:

Wordless thinking appears to exist *as a germ and as a transition*. Perhaps it is in this worldless thinking that the decisive step of cognition— the jump towards novelty, the inception, the original, anticipatory comprehension—takes place. [62, p. 415]

And finally, one more almost exclusively right-hemispheric competency must be mentioned here, one that can hardly be considered surprising in view of the ability of that side of our brain for perceiving and constructing totalities—namely, music competency [15, pp. 142–45]. How do we grasp musical structures, how do we retain themes of symphonic length, and, above all, how can we account for the emotional intensity, depth, and clarity of memories which are evoked by certain melodies? In imperial China, with its emphasis on all-pervading, rigidly defined order, music was supposed to be a prerogative of the state and thus barred from individual pursuits. Also Plato ascribes subversive properties to music:

. . . for any musical innovation is full of danger to the whole State, and ought to be prohibited. So Damon tells me, and I can quite believe him;—he says when modes of music change, the fundamental laws of the state always change with them. [86, IV, 424 C]

And in a similar vein Jean Cocteau warns of that kind of music "which one listens to with the face buried in one's hands."

In its evocative *pars-pro-toto* function, music is surpassed only by the above-mentioned olfactory sensations, and here, too, it would be an exercise in futility to attempt a translation into the digital language of the left half of our brain.*

Experiments show that music is processed almost exclusively by the right hemisphere, at least when it comes to what may be loosely called immediate musical experience. In musically trained listeners—that is, individuals who in addition to "naive" listening have learned to pay attention to such details as harmonics, orchestration, and the like—a specialized left-hemispheric ability to analyze music appears to have developed. [14, p. 51]

It follows from the above that lesions of the right hemisphere lead to disturbances in the perception of images, patterns, spatial proportions, and, generally, *Gestalten*. Such patients may be incapable of copying geometric figures, or of recognizing faces

---

* On the other hand, Richard Strauss is supposed to have once boasted that he could express anything—even a glass of foaming beer—in music.

(even their own); the ability to synthesize and integrate may be impaired or lost altogether. In his book *The Double Brain*, Dimond [21, pp. 188–89] mentions several studies which show that lesions of the right half of the brain can also impair the execution of sequential processes (for example, dressing), which—I assume—have become quite automatic as a result of numerous stereotypical repetitions and were probably stored as right-hemispheric subroutines, recallable at will before the lesion.

4

Experimental Evidence

$\mathbb{T}$HE LITERATURE dealing with the phenomena of hemispheric asymmetry and specialization, on which the preceding remarks in Chapter 3 are based, is by now quite extensive.* In this chapter, I will mention only some of those studies and investigations that have immediate relevance to my topic and provide concrete support for the general information presented in the foregoing.

As we have seen, patients who are suffering from severe lesions of one hemisphere or who have undergone commissurotomy (the disconnection of the two halves of the brain by means of surgical severance of the *corpus callosum*) may give the superficial impression of normalcy. Only detailed exploration will reveal their handicaps but, once revealed, these handicaps then permit very important conclusions to be drawn. Geschwind found, for in-

* For this reason, it is difficult to offer the interested reader a selection of basic, introductory readings. However, without any claim to completeness, the works mentioned in references 21, 23, 44, and 70 will certainly be found useful.

stance, that some individuals with extensive left-hemispheric lesions (destruction of the left visual cortex and of the splenium of the *corpus callosum*) were, among other things, unable to read words and to name Arabic numerals, but had no difficulty with Roman numerals. One may assume that this is due to the fact that Roman figures are predominantly analogic, while there is no conceivable analogy between the (digital) Arabic numerals and the concepts of quantity expressed by them. "It is important," writes Geschwind, "to realize that two tasks which appear quite similar, such as reading a word and reading a number, may in fact be carried out in quite different ways by the nervous system" [47, p. 107].

In the case of a patient with commissurotomy, Geschwind [47, p. 105] found that the individual could correctly name an object (for example, spoon, scissors, paper clip) if it was placed—concealed from his vision—into his right (left-hemispheric) hand, while he committed errors in naming those objects which he could touch (again without being able to see them) only with his left hand. Geschwind, however, discovered that, in spite of the mistaken *naming*, the patient had correctly *perceived* the object, for 1. he handled it correctly; 2. he could with his left hand select the object afterwards from a collection of diverse objects, making the selection either tactilely or visually; and 3. he could draw with his left hand the object that he had held in that hand. But he was unable to do the same (that is, use his right hand to select and/or draw the object) with regard to an object that—concealed from his vision—he had held only in his left hand. It seems to me that this experiment alone already permits very interesting conclusions about the communicational accessibility of a given hemisphere and therefore also about the "language" (in the widest sense) that needs to be used in order to reach it. Obviously, in the case of this patient, speech as a means of communication could not be utilized in some of the tasks mentioned. In his detailed article, complete with a very exhaustive bibliography and dealing with the fundamental implications for psychiatry of hemispheric specialization, David Galin, an investigator at the Langley Porter Neuropsychiatric Institute in San Francisco, describes a film taken by his colleague Roger Sperry at the California Institute of Technology in Pasadena. In one section of the film a commissurotomized patient is seen copying a colored geometric design with a set of painted blocks:

The film shows the left hand (right hemisphere) quickly carrying out the task. Then the experimenter disarranges the blocks and the right hand (left hemisphere) is given the task; slowly and with great apparent indecision, it arranges the pieces. In trying to match a corner of the design, the right hand corrects one of the blocks, and then shifts it again, apparently not realizing it was correct: the viewer sees the left hand dart out, grab the block to restore it to the correct position—and then the arm of the experimenter reaches over and pulls the intruding left hand off-camera. [42, p. 574]

The problems arising out of the disconnection of the two halves of the brain are, of course, not limited to the hands. For instance, images falling into the left half of our visual field are projected almost entirely to the right hemisphere and vice versa. That this fact may force us to revise our present view of the mechanism of repression is evidenced by another segment of Sperry's film. A commissurotomized patient is being tested with a tachistoscopic arrangement which permits the projection of images into the right or the left half of her visual field, respectively. She can name or describe the pictures flashed onto the right (left-hemispheric, verbal) half, but cannot express verbally those perceived in the left (right-hemispheric, "mute") half:

In the series of neutral geometrical figures being presented at random to the right and left fields, a nude pin-up was included and flashed to the right (nonverbal) hemisphere. The girl blushes and giggles. Sperry asks, "What did you see?" She answers, "Nothing, just a flash of light," and giggles again, covering her mouth with her hand. "Why are you laughing then?" asks Sperry, and she laughs again and says, "Oh, Dr. Sperry, you have some machine!" The episode is very suggestive; if one did not know her neurosurgical history, one might see this as a clear example of perceptual defense and think that she was "repressing" the perception of the conflictful sexual material—and even her final response (a socially acceptable *nonsequitur*) was convincing. [42, pp. 573–74]

Mutatis mutandis, the same goes for our hearing. Gordon [51], as well as Kimura [69], found that our ears transmit their information primarily to the contralateral ear, and the same appears to be the case with the nostrils and olfaction. Sperry reports:

When odors are presented through the right nostril to the minor hemisphere, the subject is unable to name the odor but can frequently tell whether it is pleasant or unpleasant. The subject may even grunt, make aversive reactions or exclamations like "phew!" to a strong unpleasant smell, but not be able to state verbally whether it is garlic, cheese, or some decayed matter. Again it appears that the affective component gets across to the speaking hemisphere, but not the more specific information. [107, p. 732]*

As can be expected, the impairment of interhemispheric integration produced by the surgical separation of the two halves of the brain gives rise to conflicts and interference phenomena. To quote Sperry again:

The minor hemisphere also commonly triggers emotional reactions of displeasure in the course of ordinary testing. This is evidenced in the frowning, wincing, and negative head shaking in test situations where the minor hemisphere, knowing the correct answer but unable to speak, hears the major hemisphere making obvious verbal mistakes. The

---

* Further information about this subject can be found in Gordon and Sperry [52]. It is interesting that, according to Indian Yoga texts, breathing exercises through the right and the left nostril, respectively, have very different effects.

minor hemisphere seems to express genuine annoyance at the errone-ous vocal responses of its better half. [107, p. 732]

Further information concerning the subject of in-terhemispheric conflict is provided by Gazzaniga [44, p. 142], who mentions a personal communication from his British col-league MacKay, who also found that the right hemisphere si-lently monitors and, if necessary, corrects the decisions and utter-ances of the left.

A large number of additional observations and research results could be presented to support these and similar assumptions. I believe, however, that the material presented so far permits the following summary:

The observable consequences of the hemispheric discon-nection of the human brain show that we actually possess two brains which can function independently of each other. As a result of this duality, they may not only not react in an identical fashion to environmental stimuli, but each of them will respond only to those external influences which fall into the domain of its competence. From this it follows that any attempt to influence either the one or the other brain must be made in that hemi-sphere's specific "language" in order for the signal or com-munication to be received and processed.

To all of this one could object that these findings, interesting as they may be, are all based on the study of severely handicapped patients in whom the coordination normally existing between the two hemispheres is greatly impaired or even lost as a result of in-jury or surgical intervention. But here, as elsewhere in brain research, it is these impairments that permit important conclu-sions to be drawn with regard to normal functioning.

What then is the nature of the relation existing between the two hemispheres under normal conditions—that is, when they are able to communicate and thus cooperate with each other? The ideal case is not difficult to imagine. It is indirectly expressed in the above-mentioned quotation from Gauss: "The solution I already know, what now remains to be done is to find the way by which I have arrived at it." In other words, the right hemisphere has already grasped the result immediately and holistically; it is now the turn of the left hemisphere, with its specialization for detailed, stepwise investigation, to supply the proof. It is not too far-fetched to assume that under normal conditions the two hemispheres reach their high degree of integration and complementarity, not in spite of, but because of, their very different specializations, and that, moreover, in any given situation the lead will be taken—so to speak—by that half of the brain which as a result of its specialization is more competent than the other to deal with the problem. So much for the ideal case.

Galin [42, p. 575] cites two further patterns of hemispheric interaction which, however, already contain the germ of conflict or interference even in the normal, unimpaired brain:

1. For the one pattern, he introduces the term "resolution by speed," meaning by it that the hemisphere that solves the problem first will gain dominance over the efferent pathways and with it the problem-solving behavior.

2. Hemispheric dominance in monkeys—which, as mentioned, is very rudimentary and therefore much more flexible than in man—can be influenced by instrumental reinforcements. As Gazzaniga [45] reports, this leads to increasing dominance of that hemisphere which is more successful in securing rewards. Since in man, too, the hemispheres are much less differentiated in childhood than in later life,* it may be assumed

* Elsewhere Gazzaniga mentions that "when the natural language and speech system is not functioning, perceptually stored information encoded at that time is not subsequently available to the language system upon its return to normal operation," and ar-

that similar reinforcements, promoting eventual dominance, may also take place between parent and infant (and—as I am tempted to add—may indeed lead by way of a self-fulfilling prophecy to one of a pair of twins becoming the "intellectual" and the other the "artist"). For this pattern of hemispheric interaction, Galin proposes the term "resolution by motivation": The hemisphere for which a certain outcome is more important will take the initiative and determine the problem-solving behavior.

But if it is true that under conditions of normal integration the lead is taken by that hemisphere which as a result of its specialization is more competent to cope with a given situation, it follows that we experience the kaleidoscopic complexity of the world in two very different ways and that these two modes of cognition are not only not interchangeable, but that it may not even be possible to translate from the one into the other. Charles Darwin seems to have been painfully aware of the impoverishment that—as we would today tend to explain it—may be the result of an excessive dominance of the left hemisphere. In his *Autobiography* he complains that

   . . . I have also almost lost my taste for pictures or music. . . .
My mind seems to have become a kind of machine for grinding general laws out of large collections of fact, but why this should have caused the atrophy of that part of the brain alone, on which the higher tastes depend, I cannot conceive. A man with a mind more highly organised or better constituted than mine, would not, I suppose, have

----

rives at a conclusion that sheds new light on the notorious difficulty of evoking childhood memories:

   In a way it is like the common experience of being unable to remember events earlier than the age of two or three. It is possible that the brain can remember critical events, which may later play a role in the control of behavior, but because the remembered events occurred prior to the clear establishment of the language system they cannot subsequently be recalled through the system. [46, p. 315]

thus suffered; and if I had to live my life again, I would have made a rule to read some poetry and listen to some music at least once every week; for perhaps the parts of my brain now atrophied would thus have been kept active through use. The loss of these tastes is a loss of happiness, and may possibly be injurious to the intellect, and more probably to the moral character, by enfeebling the emotional part of our nature.

And Galin very ably points to the difficulty of translating from the one hemispheric "language" into the other when he writes that

for example, parts of the experience of attending a symphony concert are not readily expressed in words, and the concept "democracy requires informed participation" is hard to convey in images. [42, p. 576]

And here, as already suggested, lies the potential for conflict and pathology.* There is every reason to assume that the *in-*

---

* That even under the best of circumstances there may exist an antagonistic relation between the two hemispheres is suggested by the following study. Domhoff [22], using 158 college freshmen and sophomores, conducted an inquiry into their ideas of the concepts "right" and "left" by means of a semantic differential test (a method by which the meaning of a concept is rated against a list of opposite meanings which have no factual, but a very likely subjective-associative, relation to the concept). In Domhoff's experiment, 80 subjects were tested on the concept "right" and 78 on "left." Since this method requires naming, defining, and associating, it obviously addresses itself to the left hemisphere, and the result is hardly surprising: "Right" was defined as good, light, sacred, male, clean, day, east, straight, erect, heterosexual, strong, commonplace, high, beautiful, white, correct, and life. "Left" meant just the opposite—it was characterized as bad, dark, profane, female, unclean, night, west, curved, limp, homosexual, weak, mysterious, low, ugly, black, incorrect, and death. In absence of a comparable test, engaging the right hemisphere, we have unfortunately no idea as to how this silent sufferer would express itself about its better half.

In Plato's *Republic* there is a passage in which Socrates explains to Glaucon the inferiority of those qualities of the mind that let themselves be deceived by *mimesis*, the art of deliberate make-believe:

Thus every sort of confusion is revealed within us; and this is that weakness of the human mind on which the art of conjuring and of deceiving by light and shadow and other ingenious devices imposes, having an effect upon us like magic.—True.—And the arts of measuring and numbering and weighing come to the rescue of the human understanding—there is the beauty of them—and the apparent greater or less, or more

35

*ter*hemispheric connections via the *corpus callosum* are rather scarce compared to the *intra*hemispheric connectivity, and that in certain critical situations the two hemispheres may become *functionally* separated and enter into conflict with each other—a thesis which Pierre Janet proposed almost a hundred years ago in his theory of dissociation and which was recently postulated and exemplified by Hoppe [58] for psychosomatic disturbances.*

What are such "critical situations"? It may be assumed that a functional commissurotomy is most likely to be produced by inconsistent or contradictory communications, thus creating an impasse of the kind that was first studied by the Bateson group in Palo Alto. The following is an often-quoted example from their original paper, "Toward a Theory of Schizophrenia," highlighting this communicational predicament:

A young man who had fairly well recovered from an acute schizophrenic episode was visited in the hospital by his mother. He was glad to see her and impulsively put his arm around her shoulders, whereupon she stiffened. He withdrew his arm and she asked, "Don't you love me any more?" He then blushed, and she said, "Dear, you must not be so easily embarrassed and afraid of your feelings." The patient was able to stay with her only a few minutes more and following her departure he assaulted an aide and was put in the tubs. [10]

Obviously, there exists a glaring contradiction between the mother's verbal and her nonverbal messages. But since these two

---

or heavier, no longer have the mastery over us, but give way before calculation and measure and weight?—Most true.— . . . And that which is opposed to them is one of the inferior principles of the soul?—No doubt. [86, Book X, 602 D–E]

And as the dialogue proceeds, Plato lets his Socrates become more and more outspoken in his criticism of all imagery because its nature cannot be measured, weighed, and subjected to reason.

* In connection with this subject, Bakan [6] mentions the Italian researcher Carlo Berlucchi (whose work I was unable to obtain), who found that electrical activity via the *corpus callosum* in sleeping cats drops almost to zero when the animals enter into a rapid eye movement (dream) phase.

modes of communication are processed separately by the son's two hemispheres—the mother's words by the left, her (analogic) body language by the right half of his brain—and defy integration by yielding two incompatible images of the reality aspect *mother*, the son is left with recourse to one of the following two alternatives only:

1. One hemisphere inhibits the other and thereby gains control of the efferent pathways. This amounts to a repression of the contradictory perception. The price to be paid for this solution consists in a massive falsification of reality. If it is the right hemisphere that gains over the left, the son's reactions—his behavior in general, his language and its underlying thinking processes—are likely to have unmistakable right-hemispheric (primary process) connotations and will, therefore, be archaic, metaphorical, impulsive, illogical, in a word: *psychotic*. If, however, the left hemisphere prevails, the outcome will most probably be constrained, perhaps even compulsive, but in any case emotionally flat, "cerebral" behavior.

2. If the contradiction is not swept under the rug by the pseudosolution of a repression, one could imagine that in their fight over the access to the output (efferent) channels the two hemispheres may paralyze each other, and that the resulting polarization may eventually (as in the above-mentioned example) explode into panic or a violent abreaction.

It seems to me that even this brief summary, determined by the scope of this book (and the limits of my competence), suggests that the results of the clinical and experimental studies of hemispheric functioning and cerebral asymmetry provide us with a much more comprehensive explanation of basic mental processes than the more traditional hypotheses. *Above all, they represent an important amplification of our knowledge of the behavioral (pragmatic) effects of communication.*

In the past, many researchers and clinicians, who in principle felt favorably inclined toward the postulates of pragmatics, were critical of the fact that it seemed to remain "on the surface," since it considered the mind as a *black box*, about whose inner functioning nothing was known directly—all that could be known was based on the study of the mind's input-output relations (the difference between the signals received and sent; for example, between stimulus and reaction). It was furthermore considered regretable—if not frankly unacceptable—that the pragmatics of human communication could not only not be reconciled with the traditional intrapsychic hypotheses of mental functioning, but in many respects stands in flat contradiction to them.*

The hemispheric theory now confronts us with the possibility that the conceptual distinction of conscious and unconscious processes (and with it all the manifold consequences for our understanding of psychopathology and psychotherapy that necessarily follow from this distinction) may have to be modified. We are led to the assumption that we have two conscious minds which, ideally, are capable of harmonious, complementary integration for the purpose of grasping and mastering our outer and inner reality, but which, if and when conflict arises, may be unable to communicate with each other for lack of a common language. This—as mentioned briefly in the foregoing—would be a modern confirmation of the theory of dissociation which Pierre Janet [61] postulated almost a hundred years ago at the Salpêtrière. As is known, his assumption of a *vertical* separation of the mind (and its importance as a basic element in the etiology of the neuroses†)

---

* This dissatisfaction is perhaps especially noticeable in the field of family psychotherapy, where attempts are often made to integrate the antithetical relation between the psychodynamic (intrapsychic) and the system-oriented (interactional) views into an all-embracing synthesis.

† In Janet's view, hysteria, for instance, was a "disturbance of personal synthesis."

Experimental Evidence

was soon replaced by a general acceptance of Freud's *horizontal topography of the psychic apparatus.*

The importance of all this for psychotherapy will be examined in the following chapter.

---

* Of great interest in this connection is Starobinski's study, *La relation critique* [The Critical Relation] [110], especially the chapter entitled "Freud, Breton, Myers," in which he deals with the polarity between psychoanalysis and surrealism. While the surrealists originally welcomed psychoanalysis as the way to the attainment of their main goal— man's liberation from a mostly intellectual awareness of reality and through it the synthesis of science, dream and art—Freud seems to have been embarrassed by this hope. On 26 December 1932, in his third letter to André Breton, the main spokesman of the surrealists, Freud makes it very clear that he does not understand the goal of surrealism and closes the door to further discussions by the statement that this lack of understanding lies with him, *"qui suis si eloigné de l'art"* (I, who am so removed from art). And in his letter of 20 July 1938 to Stefan Zweig, he describes his meeting with Salvador Dali and refers to the surrealists, "who seem to have chosen me as their patron saint," as "absolute fools."

In the same essay Starobinski shows how the concepts of surrealism can be traced to the thinking of Janet, Charcot, and Liébeault, rather than to the tradition running from Mesmer to Freud.

5

World Images

> What all have foreseen
> From the outset,
> And yet in the end it takes place,
> This idiocy,
> The fire it's too late to extinguish,
> Called Fate.
>
> —Max Frisch, *The Fire Raisers*

PSYCHOTHERAPY is concerned with change. But opinions differ widely about what it is supposed to change, and these divergences have their roots in the widely different views about the nature of man—and thus in a question that is philosophical, even metaphysical, and not just psychopathological. However, a *practical* answer needs to be found before we can examine the conclusions to be drawn from the foregoing as they concern the technique of therapeutic communication.

For the time being, I want to answer the question as pragmatically as possible: Anybody seeking our help suffers, in one way or another, from his relation to the world. Let this mean—borrowing from as far back as early Buddhism which, as we know, was eminently pragmatic—that he suffers from his *image* of the world, from the unresolved contradiction between the way things appear to him and the way they *should be* according to his world image. He then can choose one of two alternatives: He can intervene actively in the course of events and adapt the world more or less to his image; or, where the world cannot be changed, he can adapt his image to the unalterable facts. The first alternative may very well be the object of advice and counselling, but less likely of therapy in the more traditional sense, whereas the latter is more specifically the task and the goal of therapeutic change.*

* Here, too, some very modern-sounding antique views on this subject can be found. In his *Topica*, Aristotle already draws the fundamental distinction between self-evident conclusions which follow from the nature of things, and others which are based on generally accepted opinions and are thus essentially dialectic:

> Things are true and primary which command belief through themselves and not through anything else; . . . Generally accepted opinions, on the other hand, are those which commend themselves to all or to the majority or to the wise. [4, 100b]

And Kopperschmidt, commenting on this passage, points out that "the 'truth' of dialectic premises is linked to their validity which, in turn, can only be established through *agreement between the communicating partners*" [72, p. 127, italics mine]. This, however, means that the reasons of human action defy scientific objectification; thus Aristotle, in his *Nichomachean Ethics* [2, 1104a], argues that these reasons vary with the subject at hand, and that in practical matters and questions of expediency there are no invariable laws or scientifically established rules or even traditional maxims.

But if the realities that need to be changed cannot be grasped objectively—and there always exists the possibility that things may ultimately be quite different from the way we see them—what then shall our guidelines be? It is at this juncture that Aristotle recommends *deliberation* as a practical expedient:

> Deliberation is then employed in matters which, though subject to rules that generally hold good, are uncertain in their issue; or where the issue is indeterminate, and where, when the matter is important, we take others into our deliberations, distrusting our own capacity to decide. And we deliberate not about ends, but about means . . . [taking] some end for granted, and consider how and by what means it can be achieved. [2, 1112b]

Deliberation is thus a search for problem solutions. But to engage in this search one must know the dialectic premises (see above) which lead to the problem in the first place.

This world image, the "should" state of the world, is a peculiar thing in its own right, about which Epictetus says in his often-quoted, incomparably pithy aphorism: "It is not the things themselves that worry us, but the opinions that we have about those things."* We are thus faced with two "Realities": One that is thought to exist objectively, "out there" and independently from us (which shall be referred to as first-order reality), and one which is the result of our "opinions" and our thinking, which thus constitutes our *image* of the first and may be called second-order reality.† "The world," says Jaspers, "is the way it is. Not the world, only our knowledge can be true or false" [62, p. 627]. That the world *per se* is not accessible to direct cognition is, of course, a point which already Hume and Kant argued convincingly. Thus if we talk about and suffer from "reality," we mean a construct whose origin and premises are likely to be known to the good Lord only; a construct of which we have forgotten—if we ever knew it— that we are ourselves its architects and which we now experience "out there" as a supposedly independent, "real " reality [115].‡ Or, to repeat the bluntly Helvetian terms of the chorus

---

Viehweg [113] comes closest to the subject of this book when he refers to *Topica* as a search for premises—that is, for the sum total of the assumptions, suppositions, expectations, the image of the world as the world *should be*, without which the problem would not exist.

* Even young Marx got caught up in this contradiction. For him, however, it is merely one of the basic shortcomings of idealism. In a letter written to his father in 1837, he practices self-criticism about one of his essays on jurisprudence and explains: "I was greatly disturbed by the conflict between what actually is and what ought to be, which is peculiar to idealism."

† That it is not the "things," but what is communicated *about* these things that creates a reality is well borne out by Schneider's remark: "Rockets will deter only if words make it believable that these rockets may be fired." [98, p. 109]

‡ All I have done so far is to describe in very general terms what has been expressed so much better by Adler [1], with his concept of a *life plan*, by Piaget [83] in terms of developmental psychology, by Kelly in his *Psychology of Personal Constructs* [68], by Bateson in his essay on world images [9], by Berger and Luckman [12] in sociological terms, and especially by my friend Heinz von Foerster [34, 35] on the basis of his cybernetic epistemology.

World Images

in Max Frisch's play *The Fire Raisers*, from which the epigraph of this chapter was taken: "This idiocy, the fire it's too late to extinguish, called Fate."

We must think of a world image, then, as the most comprehensive, most complex synthesis of the myriads of experiences, convictions, and influences, of their interpretations, of the resulting ascription of value and meaning to the objects of perception, which an individual can muster. The world image is, in a very concrete and immediate sense, the outcome of communication, as I have tried to show elsewhere [115]. It is not *the world*, but a mosaic of single images which may be interpreted in one way today and differently tomorrow; a pattern of patterns; an interpretation of interpretations; the result of incessant decisions about what may and what may not be included in these meta-interpretations, which themselves are the consequences of past decisions.*

Nietzsche already knew of the life-sustaining or life-threatening power of world images when he stated that he who has a *why* of living will endure almost any *how*. And an experiment (of which I was unfortunately only able to obtain hearsay knowledge, but which sounds quite believable) suggests that animals too depend on their world images, for better or for worse: It would appear that rats that fall into water will die long before reaching the state of final physical exhaustion if by swimming around they have "convinced" themselves that there is no way of saving themselves by climbing out. But if such a rat is picked out of the water in time, this rescue leads to a decisive change in its "world image." Instead of giving up and drowning

---

* Whatever his "reasons," the depressed patient selects out of the world that misery which we, too, could (but do not) utilize for the construction of our second-order reality. On the other hand, my dog and my cat live with world images which appear to be quite adequate not only for their survival, but also their well-being, yet would be totally insufficient for me.

upon realization of the hopelessness of the situation, it will, when the experiment is repeated, continue to swim until total exhaustion. If it were a human being, it would hardly be absurd to suppose that it was the belief that a higher, saving power would rescue him again that enabled him to hold on to life until the last moment. In oncology (the study of tumors), evidence seems to be accumulating that those cancer patients who in an apparently "immature" attitude are unwilling to come to terms with the fact of being ill, who hate their illness and stubbornly reject the idea of death, have a better prognosis than those who prepare themselves for death with mature equanimity. (More about this subject on pages 61–62.)

All of these considerations may strike one as highly questionable, especially if one rejects them in typical left-hemispheric *hubris* as imprecise and pseudophilosophical. But far from considering them trivial, even a genius like Schrödinger saw in them a fundamental issue: "Every man's world picture is and always remains a construct of his mind and cannot be proved to have any other existence" [99, p. 44]. World images are inaccessible to orthodox scientific objectification, because they must of necessity include their author (the observer or describer), and this leads into the well-known problems of paradoxical self-reflexiveness. "All that is true resides in the separation of subjectivity and objectivity," postulates Jaspers and goes on to say:

To be sure, when doing scientific research there is in us the constant impulse of looking at the world as if I, the recognizing agent, were not in it and with it; we would like to explore the world by excluding the fact that it is we who take cognizance of it. [62, p. 628]

And again:

Through the act of cognition the world arranges itself, as it were, into given world images. Especially the modern world images of the exact

natural sciences tended to convey the suggestion that in them the world
can be seen in its entirety and its actual reality . . . But critical science
has just the effect of making world images disintegrate. [62, p. 91]*

A totally subject-free world, that is, a world from which all
subjectivity would be banished in deference to the scientific
dogma of absolute objectivity, could—if such an objectification
were at all possible—not be perceived and would thus defy investigation. Von Foerster points to this paradoxical situation when
he stresses:

. . . a description of the universe implies one who describes it (observes
it). What we need now is the description of the "describer" or, in other
words, we need a theory of the observer. Since to the best of available
knowledge it is only living organisms which would qualify as being ob-
servers, it appears that this task falls to the biologist. But he himself is a
living being, which means that in his theory he has not only to account
for himself, but also for his writing this theory. This is a new state of affairs in scientific discourse for, in line with the traditional viewpoint
which separates the observer from his observations, reference to this discourse was to be carefully avoided. [35, p. 1]

And Schrödinger already explained:

The reason why our sentient, percipient and thinking ego is met
nowhere within our scientific world picture can easily be indicated in
seven words: because it is itself that world picture. It is identical with the
whole and therefore cannot be contained in it as a part of it. [99, p. 52]

We are now at the point where the two main themes developed
so far—hemispheric asymmetry and the concept of the world
image—may be brought together. *The translation of the perceived*

---

* Compare with this the very different assumption of classical epistemology, as it
reflects itself, for instance, in Freud's confident remark: "At least in the older and more
mature sciences, there is even to-day a solid ground work which is only modified and
improved, but no longer demolished." [39]

reality, this synthesis of our experience of the world into an image, is most probably the function of the right hemisphere. To the left half, presumably, goes the task of rationalizing this image, of separating the whole (the *pleroma* in Greek philosophy) into subject and object, of the reification of reality as well as the task of drawing (in accordance with the words of the chorus in *The Fire Raisers*) the now seemingly inescapable consequences. They, in turn, consolidate the image in self-fulfilling, self-validating ways to the point where whatever may contradict the image no longer leads to its correction but to its further refinement and elaboration.*

To change this seemingly unchangeable reality, one needs to know first *what* has to be changed (which means that one must grasp the world image in question), and secondly, *how* this change can be practically achieved. (Note the absence of the question *why?*; that is, of the causal, past-oriented uncovering—in short, the depth-psychological approach to human problems.) From these two foci, the *what* and the *how*, there follow important conclusions for the *language* and the *technique* of psychotherapy.

As far as the *language* is concerned, it should now be clear that—like Monsieur Jourdain and his prose—we have always known it. It is the language of the right hemisphere. In it the world image is conceived and expressed, and it is, therefore, the

---

* Gerald Holton, a leading authority on the history of science and the author of a method of thematic analysis of scientific world images, has been able to show the existence of this problem in the lives of great scientists. According to him, certain themes develop very early in life and may then exert a determining influence for a long time. In a recent interview at Stanford University, he explained it as follows:

It is during such episodes as these [for example, when Einstein was given a magnet at age 4 or 5] that the scientific imagination gets formed and that a commitment to a thema comes about. Such a commitment can be changed in later life, but that seems difficult to do. Usually the decision is made early, is found to be useful, and persists a long time, *even in the face of contrary evidence.* [57, italics mine]

key to our being in, and our suffering in relation to, the world.

But if this is so, then it also reveals the inappropriateness of a procedure which essentially consists in translating this analogic language into the digital language of explanation, argument, analysis, confrontation, interpretation, and so forth, * and which, through this translation, repeats the mistake which made the sufferer seek help in the first place—instead of learning the patient's right-hemispheric language and utilizing it as the royal road to therapeutic change.*

As regards *technique*, there are three approaches which in the practice of psychotherapy offer themselves in varying degrees and combinations:

1. The use of right-hemispheric language patterns;
2. Blocking the left hemisphere;
3. Specific behavior prescriptions.

So important are these three possibilities that they shall now be dealt with in separate chapters.

---

* Cf. Starobinski:

. . . when the rationalistic activity of psychoanalysis turns to dreams or neurotic symptoms—and especially when it turns to the musings of the poets—it consists in a reading and a translation: It has to do with passing from one language into the other, from the enigmatic language of the symbols into the clear language of interpretation; this presupposes an art of deciphering and decoding, based on a knowledge of the vocabulary, the grammar, the syntax, the rhetoric of that language in which—between unconsciousness and consciousness—the wish expresses itself. And in the measure that the reading progresses there diminishes the part of the mystery. [110, p. 269]

Let it be noted already here that interpretation as a form of therapeutic communication is thus a "one way" translation, from the unconscious to the conscious, and that it entails a loss of that information for which there are no equivalents in left-hemispheric language.

6

Right-Hemispheric Language Patterns

Facts have their own pronunciation—
in every language a different one.
—*Vieslav Brudzinski*

WE NOW COME to purely practical considerations. As
explained in the Preface, this book wants to be a cross between a
grammar and a language course, and therefore it cannot possibly
give a catalogue of the most appropriate linguistic interventions
which are to be applied in any given therapy situation. A grammar, it will be remembered, cannot (and is not meant to) list all
the word combinations (sentences) which are possible in a language. Rather, its purpose is to make transparent the rules which,
when grasped and followed, will permit the free construction of
any (admissible) sentence. But since these rules can best be dem-
onstrated by examples, and since in this book the latter are supposed to highlight the strange "grammar" of the right hemi-

sphere, the frame of these exemplifications should not be drawn too narrowly. Let me repeat the purpose of this and the following chapters: they are designed to promote the *understanding* of rules; their *application* must necessarily be left to the skill, the inventiveness, and the presence of mind of the therapist, and to the unique circumstances of every given situation.

I shall, however, borrow heavily from the field of hypnosis, and especially from the truly unique teachings of Dr. Milton H. Erickson. Hypnosis is a field in which the ability to apply very specific language forms is decisive while at the same time—to quote from the introduction to his recently published work *Hypnotic Realities*—it consists in "carefully planned extensions of some everyday processes of normal living." [31] But these language forms have hardly been investigated until recently.*
Other examples in the present book are taken from general, everyday language, but their structure can be applied directly to the language of therapy. In comparison to anecdotal or casuistic exemplifications from actual therapy sessions, they have the advantage of not requiring long explanations of background and context. The division of this chapter's contents into several sub-headings is intended to contribute to a more systematic manner of presentation.

CONDENSATIONS

A startling example for the minimum of digital language that is still sufficient even in our modern, highly complex world was provided by the trial of the French farmer Gaston Domenici, as

---

* Erickson's work, especially its linguistic components, has lately been studied in great detail by Bandler and Grinder. [7; 8]

described by Jean Giono. Domenici was accused of having murdered, on 5 August 1952, near his farm at Lurs in Haute Provence, the British scientist Sir Jack Drummond, his wife, and their little daughter. With regard to the language of the accused, a 71-year-old patriarch who ruled his family with an iron hand, Giono has this to say:

The accused . . . , in order to express himself, indeed to defend his own head, commands a vocabulary of no more than thirty to forty words. [48, p. 62]

One could, of course, argue that this is the rather special case of a very "primitive" man whose communicative skills never evolved beyond an absolute minimum. But what Giono shows, among other things, is that every once in a while even this incredible minimum turns into the vehicle of rich significance—for example, when Domenici's archaic concept of honor is challenged or when he tries to explain to the Court (which to him must have seemed an authority from another planet) his being-in-the-world. Giono reports that:

. . . he begins, at one point, by saying: "Me, I was grabbed like a sheep in a sheep-fold," and then goes on to speak six perfect sentences describing his life as a solitary shepherd. I glance at my friends. We are flabbergasted. So much so that I forget to take these sentences down. I regret it. [48, p. 75]

Domenici personifies one extreme, the minimum. The other extreme of language, the extent of its richness, is utterly fantastic—indeed astronomic. How many of us are aware of what Farb puts so eloquently:

Not every human being can play the violin, do calculus, jump high hurdles, or sail a canoe, no matter how excellent his teachers or how arduous his training—but every person constantly creates utterances never before spoken on earth. Incredible as it may seem at first thought, the sentence you just read possibly appeared in exactly this form for the first time in the history of the English language—and the same thing might be said about the sentence you are reading now. In fact, if conventional remarks—such as greetings, farewells, stock phrases like *thank you*, proverbs, clichés, and so forth—are disregarded, in theory all of a person's speech consists of sentences never before uttered. [33]*

But here lies the rub. We may be able to construct countless sentences never uttered before; their essential meaning, however, may vary little or not at all over large numbers of them. In fact, verbosity is inversely related to meaning, and especially clichés are notoriously meaningless.

By contrast, the language of dreams, fairy tales and myths, of hypnosis, delusions, and other similar manifestations (the language of the right hemisphere that consequently offers itself as the most natural key to those areas of the mind in which alone therapeutic change can take place), has always been known to be particularly condensed and charged with meaning. For an example of this, we need only to remember Freud's treatment of Irma's dream in his *Interpretation of Dreams:* the dream itself takes up one paragraph, its interpretation several pages.

The enormous condensation and potentiation of meaning inherent in the deliberate use of seemingly archaic and primitive, yet at the same time uniquely expressive, language forms appears, for instance, over and over again in the work of so demonic a master of language as the Viennese writer and critic Karl Kraus. At one point, in the satirical review *Die Fackel* [The Torch], he refers to the Nazis as the *Untergangster des Abendlandes.*

* And Farb then gives some simple figures, showing how the complexity of language grows exponentially with the number of available words, and points out that "it would take 10,000,000,000,000 years (two thousand times the estimated age of the earth) to utter all the possible English sentences that use exactly twenty words." [33]

51

Younger readers may not know that Oswald Spengler's famous work, *Der Untergang des Abendlandes* [The Decline of the West], had been banned by the Nazi ideologists as a particularly despicable product of decadent philosophy.* Karl Kraus, who had never tired of warning against the dangers of Nazism for the civilized world, condensed *Untergang* (decline) and *Gangster* into the neologism *Untergangster* (under-gangster), thereby not only intimating that they were inferior even in the realm of absolute evil, but also implying that *they* represented the decline of the West, and finally giving the title of the book and its contemporary significance a totally new meaning, hoisting the Nazis by their own petard, so to speak. *Untergangster* instead of *Untergang*—four additional letters, but what a totally different sense, and how much more elegant, terse, and immediate is the effect of this condensation compared to my clumsy, cerebral analysis!

If somebody said about a vegetarian restaurant that it serves *biodeplorable food*, most of us would tend to see in it a condensation with *biodegradable*, but also a slip of the tongue through which a hidden dislike for so-called natural foods found its way into the open, and we would further be inclined to consider this slip more significant and revealing than an open, nonaccidental criticism. But there is absolutely no reason why a punster should not make deliberate use of this technique precisely for the purpose of making his point especially strongly. Similarly, in its funny terseness typical of most condensations, the term *popollution* conveys a much more immediate and powerful meaning than a well-formed sentence purporting that overpopulation is a significant source of pollution. Notice especially the phonetic similarity of population and popollution, which through its clang

---

* Exactly why this book had gained such outstanding negative honors did not have to be explained, since it was burned. The reason thus remained an enigma which mystified even its author and prompted his delightful aphorism: *"The Decline of the West*—the book of which my Führer has read the whole title."

association further enhances the effect of the condensation. Or consider the amount of (mostly nasty) meaning which is compressed into the neologism *genitalmud* for psychoanalysis: How long an explanation in rational (left-hemispheric) language would be needed to convey the same meaning?! Magi Wechsler's cartoon, *"Definition"* (below), neatly spoofs the hopelessness of

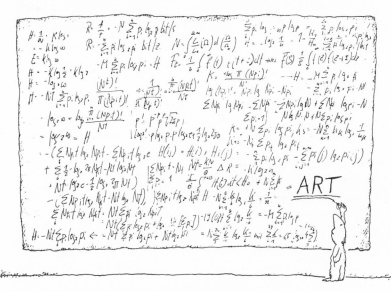

attempting to define something so undefinable as the essence of art in left-hemispheric, mathematical language.*

James Joyce, the author of innumerable such condensations and contaminations must be mentioned here at least briefly; for instance, when in *Ulysses* he talks about *syphilization* instead of civilization, or when, in *Finnegans Wake,* he leaves it up to the reader to decide whether the expression *freudful mistakes* means Freudian slips, *freudvolle* (joyful), frightful or fruitful errors. Or

---

* Of course, her cartoon has an unavoidable flaw: The word *art* is itself still a left-hemispheric symbol. But short of replacing it with, say, a painting by Marc Chagall, there is no better way of making her point.

take Arno Schmidt, the German James Joyce, whose work—like Joyce's—has Indo-European dimensions, referring to somebody as *Fuck-Totum*, or pretending to wonder whether *Hamlet spoilt by man* means "The Prince of Denmark, corrupted by mankind" or "One man ruins a small village" [97].

What in Joyce and Schmidt is an art form, in the case of the schizophrenic, with his endless word plays, puns, condensations, and switches of meaning from the literal to the metaphorical and vice versa, presumably amounts to a very useful defense against having to take a clear stand on any issue and thus becoming responsible for it. His "schizophrenese" enables him to claim at any given moment that the meaning of his communication, for which he is being criticized, is not the meaning that he meant— and he may then even proceed to wonder how anybody in his right mind could attribute to it such a distorted sense as the other just did.

These subtle nuances and shifts of meaning are also in the essence of the *joke*, another important language form whose therapeutic effect can be far above that of many a ponderous psychiatric interpretation. Evidence of the power and effect of jokes can be seen in the fact that dictators and totalitarian regimes—and occasionally also thin-skinned politicians in democracies—fear them like the plague. When one of Hitler's laudatory titles, *grösster Feldherr aller Zeiten* (greatest strategist of all times), was condensed into *Gröfaz*, it was considered a subversive act and the joke could land you in jail—proving that the combination of two things, both considered harmless in and by themselves (the reference to the Führer's military genius and the use of acrostics, as dear to the heart of the Nazis as it is nowadays universally), may be anything but harmless.* And when Mauthe refers to us Aus-

---

* The Gestapo had its own joke department (may I be forgiven this horrid non sequitur) whose task it was to trace the originators of political jokes. After all, jokes are political dynamite whose production and possession was (and in many parts of the world still is) strictly forbidden. From this point of view, it made sense to search for their underground

trians as the *Irrelevantiner des Westens* (the Irrelevanters of the West) [79], he, too, condenses into these few words a far more sarcastic meaning than a long and ultimately empty explanation could convey (to say nothing of the fact that in English the additional pun with *irre* [insane] is lost). Yet, the term is not offensive; it obeys Cicero's rule which (in Sir Thomas Hobby's Elizabethan translation) states that "jestes must bite the hearer like a sheepe, but not like a dogge."

In its sovereign disdain for the bounds of logic and rationality, the joke can explode world images and thus become the agent of change. And it, therefore, seems strange that Freud, the author of the most classic treatment of this subject—*Jokes and Their Relation to the Unconscious* [38]—conceives of the joke only as a "one-way street" *from* the unconscious to the conscious, but does not draw the—by no means far-fetched—conclusion to utilize the language of the joke in the opposite direction, namely as a means of communication *with* the unconscious. Perhaps he was too much under the persuasive power of his own maxim that where Id was, there Ego shall be. Apart from this, his book is a veritable catalogue of patterns of jokes and it not only makes for highly entertaining reading but also enables the reader to draw very useful conclusions about the potential of jokes in therapeutic communication. The same holds for three other, more recent works from an almost overwhelming number of books on the subject: Koestler's *Act of Creation* [71], Fry's *Sweet Madness* [40], and Fry and Allen's *Make 'em Laugh* [41].

As mentioned, jokes have a disrespectful ability to make light of seemingly monolithic world orders and world images.* This

---

factories. That jokes might be a spontaneous expression of the sound instinct of The People—an argument, used otherwise as a convenient and irrefutable justification for even the most hideous crimes—was left-hemispherically unthinkable.

  * An example for this effect is the joke which Victor Frankl likes to include in his talks: In the First World War an aristocratic colonel and his regimental medical officer, a Jew, are sitting in their dugout under heavy Russian shelling. The colonel looks at the doctor

may help to explain why it is that people who suffer from emotional problems are half over them once they manage to laugh at their predicament. "He laughed to free his mind from his mind's bondage," we read in *Ulysses*. Laughter appears to be the most immediate and spontaneous reaction when, after suffering through a seemingly interminable night of hopelessness and despair, we perceive the dawn of a completely unthought-of solution. After his odyssey through the Magic Theater, the hero in Hermann Hesse's *Steppenwolf* laughs out loud as he realizes that reality is nothing but the free choice of one of many doors that are open at all times. And something similar happens to the Zen pupil at the moment of his enlightenment—he laughs.

FIGURATIVE LANGUAGE

Dreaming is a manifestation of the right hemisphere.* There is an even vaster literature about the language of dreams and its meaning than about humor. And again we are surprised to find that—with one important exception—the dream, like the joke, has been considered until very recently to be a "one-way street" and that the idea of deliberately using this very language to go in

---

and says half-condescendingly, half-compassionately: "Well, admit it that you are scared. It just goes to show the inferiority of the Jewish race." And the little doctor replies: "Yes, I am really scared. But what that proves about races, I don't know. Because if you, colonel, were as scared as I am you would be running for dear life." And with this reply, which is extremely intricate from a logical point of view, he not only demolishes a prejudice, but puts the shoe on the other foot.

* Bogen [15, p. 194, footnote] reports that several of his patients ceased to dream after commissurotomy, while they had reported vivid dreams before their operation. Even if this were merely due to their inability to verbalize their dreams, it would not detract significantly from Bogen's finding. In a recent summary, Bakan [6] reports additional evidence that dreaming is a right-hemispheric function.

Right-Hemispheric Language Patterns

the opposite direction, into the right-hemisphere, in order to influence and change a world image has never been seriously considered. The one exception is, of course, hypnotherapy, which has always relied on figurative, dreamlike language, and considers its mastery a precondition for the success of therapeutic interventions.*

* However, even this very sketchy presentation must acknowledge that elements of this approach can be found in several schools of therapy. That the *expression* of the inner drama has a cathartic effect was described by Aristotle in his *Poetics*; it finds its modern application in psychodrama, Gestalt therapy, and psychosynthesis. But to a large extent these methods also deal with the expression, the abreaction, and the lifting into consciousness of elements of the inner world, and not with what this book is about—the approach from the *outside* into the *inside* through the medium of the language of the inner world.

One definite exception is John Rosen, the initiator of *Direct Analysis*, whose uncommon clinical intuition enables him to enter the delusionary world of his patients. Some of his highly imaginative and interesting techniques are described in his book *Direct Analysis* [94, especially Chapter 7].

In this connection, mention must also be made of Bruno Bettelheim's recent book, *The Uses of Enchantment*, which deals with the use of fairy tales in therapeutic dialogue. In it Bettelheim offers many examples of his observation that children (as well as the storytelling adults) will distort a fairy tale in order to adapt it to their needs and expectations. However, even for Bettelheim the fairy tale remains predominantly the expression of the inner world, offering "examples of both temporary and permanent solutions to pressing difficulties "[13], which through their millionfold recreation and evocation have assumed archetypical qualities. But Bettelheim *is* aware of the possibility of conscious, deliberate modifications of the plot of fairy tales to suit the needs of a child. He exemplifies this with a charming passage from Bettina von Arnim's book, *Goethes Briefwechsel mit einem Kinde* [Goethe's Correspondence with a Child]. Bettina quotes Goethe's mother, who recounts telling fairy tales to little Johann Wolfgang:

He devoured me with his eyes; and if the fate of one of his favorites did not go as he wished, this I could see from the anger in his face, or his efforts not to break out in tears. Occasionally he interfered by saying: "Mother, the princess will not marry the miserable tailor, even if he slays the giant," at which I stopped and postponed the catastrophe until the next evening. So my imagination often was replaced by his; and when the following morning I arranged fate according to his suggestions and said, "You guessed it, that's how it came out," he was all excited, and one could see his heart beating. [5]

A modern master in the use of the language of imagery is Milton Erickson, who is known to answer his patients' questions (above all, the typical question: "What shall I do in this situation?") with lengthy, complicated stories that, from a logical point of view, seem to have absolutely nothing to do with the subject at hand. My colleagues and I suspected for a long time that the figure of Don Juan in Carlos Castañeda's books was really

How often do we "understand" dreams? And what can one "say" about dreamlike productions, such as Buñuel's *The Discreet Charm of the Bourgeoisie* and *The Phantom of Liberty?* All we "know" is that they are not a hoax perpetrated on the public, but they somehow touch us in a manner that is difficult or impossible to describe. The same is true of art forms like those of the Viennese school of fantastic realism. While the resistance to verbal analysis is admittedly the common denominator of all representational art, these are artistic manifestations that are particularly removed from all logical, reasonable appreciation of their essential meaning. Literature is no exception. Take this example from a novel by the Swiss writer and poet Heinz Weder, a book of truly classically evocative, dreamlike language:

. . . There, three four houses, a run-down inn, I enter, the wine is unsurpassed, summer's essence, days of bronze and of black ornament, salamander gorge, I ask for some names, laughter, . . . a dog barks, the sun floats in the metallic blue of the phosphorous cliffs, the bells toll, I see the priest, black figure, black figure of ink, black figure of ink and black laughter, running across the road, greeting perfunctorily, and there he is again, in his garden. . . . [119]

This language does not explain; it creates, it evokes. Without knowing how, the reader suddenly finds himself in the depth of a summer's day noon hour, feeling, seeing, smelling, and hearing it. And now let us compare this with a passage from a trance induction by Erickson; the same language, the same structure, the same effect:

Erickson—an assumption which, upon our inquiry, he denied for once directly and not by telling a story.

Guided fantasy as a therapeutic technique is also explained very well by Bandler and Grinder in their *Structure of Magic I* [7, pp. 166–69].

Right-Hemispheric Language Patterns

And that paperweight; the filing cabinet; your foot on the rug; the ceiling light; the draperies; your right hand on the arm of the chair; the pictures on the wall; the changing focus of your eyes as you glance about; the interest of the book titles; the tension in your shoulders; the feeling of the chair; the disturbing noises and thoughts; weight of hands and feet; weight of problems, weight of desk; the stationery stand; the records of many patients; the phenomena of life, of illness, of emotion, of physical and mental behavior; the restfulness of relaxation; the need to attend to one's needs; the need to attend to one's tension while looking at the desk or the paperweight or the filing cabinet; the comfort of withdrawal from the environment; fatigue and its development; the unchanging character of the desk; the monotony of the filing cabinet; the need to take a rest; the comfort of closing one's eyes; the relaxing sensation of a deep breath; the delight of learning passively; the capacity for intellectual learning by the unconscious. [26]

One could argue that this quotation is not only devoid of the aesthetic qualities of the preceding example, but that it is mainly an empty enumeration of objects. But both Weder and Erickson use evocative languages, except that they move in opposite directions: Weder evokes from inside out by calling upon images that preexist in the reader's inner space; Erickson utilizes what is immediately, physically present in the situation and associates it with sensations and other experiences, thus proceeding from the outer into the inner world, so to speak. He achieves this by careful observation of his client's behavior and by closely tracking his perceptions: his looking around in the room; his fixing his gaze upon certain objects, which prompts Erickson to immediately mention some of their more obvious characteristics or associations ("the interest of the book titles," "weight of desk"); impressions and specific body sensations (light, the changing focus of the eyes, the feeling of the chair, the right hand on the arm of the chair, the feet on the rug, and so forth), of which it may be assumed with certainty that the client is either aware of them at that moment or that they can be brought into his awareness by simply mentioning them. There is yet another element which is exemplified in this passage from Erickson's induction and which—although not falling under the rubric of figurative language—may best be mentioned here. It is the *interspersal technique*, introduced by him into hypnotherapy, whose applicability for general (that is, nonhypnotic) psychotherapy is beyond question.

As the reader has probably noticed, the above passage not only contains references to the subject's behavior and to the objects of his immediate surroundings as well as to his body sensations, but also a number of subtle, suggestive associations to moods and ideas, such as disturbing thoughts (whose occurrence may safely be assumed), emotional tension and relaxation, attention to and withdrawal from the environment, the records of many patients and the association conveyed by them that many people with many different problems have found help in this room, and many other associations. Into the monotonous stream of these seemingly empty enumerations whose purpose, on the one hand, remains incomprehensible because of their all too obvious nature but, on the other hand, appear unimportant, there are interspersed specific suggestions, couched in the simplest possible language: "the restfulness of relaxation . . . the comfort of withdrawal . . . of closing one's eyes . . . deep breath," and so on. Or, to explain this procedure by analogy: Imagine the page of a book which seems to contain nothing but a lengthy, trivial, boring description of some unimportant matter, but on which certain words are underlined.* If only these words are read in the order of their appearance, it turns out that they give a totally dif-

---

* In hypnosis this emphasis is achieved by minimal changes in vocal pitch or volume, by preceding pauses, by uttering these words during the subject's exhalation, and by minimal gestures or similar signals.

ferent meaning than the text in which they are embedded. But the grasping of this other meaning, of this totally different *Gestalt*, is presumably the competence of the right hemisphere and the interspersal technique, therefore, a way of reaching it. (A detailed description of the technique, with extensive examples, can be found in Erickson [29]; a quotation is given on page 84 of this book.)

But back to the subject of figurative language. The power of concrete imagery has been utilized by medicine men and psychic healers for thousands of years. I have already mentioned that the suggestion of images is widely used in hypnotherapy (and in Autogenic Training). Instead of speaking a purely intellectual language to suggest, for instance, that an obese patient will lose his excessive appetite within a few days, it is much more effective to have him create in his mind as vivid and detailed as possible a picture of his body fat, whereby it remains totally irrelevant whether this picture is medically correct or not. What is essential is that it is *his* visualization, *his* picture. One may thus obtain from him a description of yellowish-white, oval cells, stacked in thick, honeycomblike layers. Next he is asked to provide a visualization of his proteins, for instance, in the shape of little animals, which will viciously attack the fat cells and devour them from within, thereby releasing the energy trapped in these cells and producing a sensation of physical comfort and heightened energy.

This type of visual concentration exercise is finding increasing recognition in the treatment of cancer,* not only in the form of suggestions for the relief of pain or of the side effects of radiation

---

* The possible role of emotional factors in the appearance of cancer and the course of the disease is being considered by many experts. Cf. the proceedings of two important conferences on the psychophysiological aspects of cancer, organized by the New York Academy of Sciences in 1966 [95] and 1969 [91], respectively.

and chemotherapy,* but with a view to influencing the course of the disease itself. In this connection, special mention must be made of the research team headed by the oncologist Simonton, whose patients are systematically trained in the use of specific exercises in visual concentration [104]. Among other tasks, the patients are encouraged to evoke visualizations that to them personally and idiosyncratically represent the most vivid and meaningful image of their illness, and this image is then gradually modified through suggestions toward remission, healing, and well-being. The patient is, for instance, requested to visualize his white blood cells as ferocious polar bears, hungrily roaming his entire body and viciously attacking any cancer cell that they can hunt up.

Erickson describes many similar interventions. Thus, in a case of frigidity he may instruct his patient to imagine in the greatest possible detail how she would go about defrosting her refrigerator. This intervention can take place either in trance or in waking state. In his slow, repetitive, monotonous style, he wonders aloud how she will approach this task, whether she will begin with the top shelf, or the bottom shelf, or perhaps in the middle. What will she take out first, what next? What might she possibly find in some corner that she has forgotten putting there and should have thrown away a long time ago? How will she go about the actual thawing, and while she is doing this, what forgotten memories or completely unrelated thoughts might perhaps come to her mind? In what order will she eventually put things back in, what will she consider worth keeping and what not? At no time will Erickson refer directly to her sexual problem; he will merely ponder in the most superficial, cumbersome way the details of this trivial household chore. Needless to say, this intervention is

---

* Cf. for instance [29] and [55].

essentially a dream "in reverse": What Erickson says could just as well be reported by the patient as her dream, in which consciously unacceptable material camouflages itself into the language of images in order to bypass the censorship of the left hemisphere. Of course, the important difference here is that the dream is usually the *passive* expression of inner conflict, while Erickson's use of dream language represents an *active* intervention.*

Poetry, too, uses figurative, pictorial language and in addition is closely related to music through the rhythm of its words. This may account for the strange power of rhymes, of which Schopenhauer remarked that "through it we are corrupted into accepting something that we would not consider valid in everyday language."†

An extremely unusual case, reported by the Italian linguist Bausani, sheds further light on the language of poetry. He studied a young Italian, E. J., who as a child had developed an ar-

---

* The above should not be construed to mean that only *visual* imaginations can be applied. As the reader probably is aware, Autogenic Training is largely based on proprioceptive fantasies. Acoustic imaginations are also known to be very effective, as illustrated by the following report of one of Erickson's patients about an imagined metronome:

When I listen to the imaginary metronome, it speeds up or slows down, gets louder or fainter, as I start to go into a trance, and I just drift along. With the real metronome, it remains distractingly constant, and it keeps pulling me back to reality instead of letting me drift along into a trance. The imaginary metronome is changeable and always fits in with just the way I'm thinking and feeling, but I have to fit myself to the real one. [25]

In musically talented persons, an induction of self-hypnosis can sometimes be achieved very effectively by having them "listen" to an imaginary melody which fully adapts itself to the depth and rhythm of the trance experience.

† Cf. also Heinrich Heine, *The Poems of Heine*, trans. Edgar Alfred Bowring (London: George Bell & Sons, 1905), p. 210.

And when I to you my grief did confide,
You only yawned, and nothing replied;
But when I reduced my sorrow to rhyme,
You praised me greatly and called it sublime.

tifical language which he called *Markuska* and which he had refined and perfected over the years. And, as in the case of the Icelandic girl, mentioned on page 5n, also E. J.'s siblings and playmates took over some of the elements of *Markuska*.

"How can such curious manifestations of linguistic inventiveness be explained?" asks Bausani. And he continues:

We believe that what is involved here is the emergence into explicit consciousness of processes which in similar, but unconscious, fashion take place in the languages of mental patients, somnambulists and spiritistic media, but it must be stressed that this young language inventor was mentally perfectly normal, although endowed from childhood with a strong inclination to learn foreign languages. Not without interest are the emotional manifestations that accompanied the emergence and the development of this "artificial" language, for instance a feeling of inner relief or complete freedom, a certain joyful mood and at times also sexual excitement. Not rarely did our young friend take recourse to his "Markuska" language in order to compose poetry. [11, p. 28]

And it is with reference to E. J.'s poetry that Bausani makes the following remarks that are of relevance to my subject:

What was "strange" about these poems was only their language, for neither in content nor in form did they deviate much from the well-known type of decadent and romantic lyrics, a genre which the author simply abhorred in his poems composed in Italian. The latter, without exception, were in the style of modern, "hermetic" poetics, devoid of rhyme and rather impersonal in content. In E. J.'s "Markuska" poetry, on the other hand, certain states of consciousness and emotions strove to poetic expression which—although E. J. did not consider them worthy of "serious" formulation—in their own way thus found a secret, half burlesque manner of expressing themselves. [11, p. 29]

It is tempting to see in E. J.'s poetic productions the separate expressions of his two hemispheres, with the left speaking the official language of reason while the right, in spite of the "abhorrence" of its better half, made itself heard through the expedient of a secret language and of irony—very much like the political joke which, as mentioned already, manages to find its "subversive" expression against the lack of humor and humanity of the ideological dogma.

It would be surprising if the advertising industry had not discovered the power of the rhyme in order to get a point across whose inanity would otherwise be patent to just about everybody. The height—or rather, the depth—is, of course, the sung commercial. Magic formulas and incantations (*abracadabra* and numerous others) were usually rhymes, and the style of many prayers, to say nothing of the monotony of litanies, draws on the suggestive power of rhyme and rhythm.

All this should not be construed to imply that the therapist must learn to express himself in rhymes, but only that here as elsewhere we should be aware of the existence of language forms that have particularly suggestive influence.

Eastern cultures are known to be particularly rich in figurative similes and metaphors, as evidenced by innumerable Russian, Jewish, Armenian, Arabic, and especially Far-Eastern stories. How much more immediate, for example, is the effect of the following parable of Chuang Tzu's than the detailed, "reasonable" interpretation of a certain conflict-engendering human attitude:

Suppose a boat is crossing a river, and another, empty boat is about to collide with it. Even an irritable man would not lose his temper. But supposing there was some one in the second boat. Then the occupant of the first would shout to him to keep clear. And if the other did not hear the first time, nor even when called to three times, bad language would inevitably follow. In the first case there was no anger, in the second there was; because in the first case the boat was empty, and in the second it was occupied. And so it is with man. If he could only roam empty through life, who would be able to injure him? [18]

Or another, allegedly true, story (whose truth or falsehood is, of course, completely irrelevant): Somewhere in the tropics monkeys are caught by means of a gourd which is tied to the ground and into which the hunters place a fruit that the animals are particularly fond of. The opening of the gourd is wide enough to permit the monkey to put his hand into it. But as soon as he grabs the fruit, he can no longer withdraw his hand with the fruit through the narrow opening. To free his hand he would have to let go of the fruit, but this he cannot do in his greed. Thus he becomes his own prisoner, for while he is unable to let go and run away, the hunters come and throw a net over him. So he is, after all, forced to release the fruit, but now it is too late.

Both stories express the same basic thought: the necessity to empty one's mind and to let go—a necessity about which one could intellectualize forever.

Finally, yet another property of figurative language must be mentioned. As already pointed out, its structure is comparatively primitive. It lacks the highly developed logical syntax of digital communication, above all the concept of *negation*—that is, words like *not, none, nobody, never, nowhere,* and so forth, which are indispensable for the direct expression of the notions of nonexistence, absence, nonapplicability, and the like. As explained elsewhere [116, pp. 98–105], it is difficult, if not impossible, to represent the nonoccurrence of an event by a picture. The sentence, *The man plants a tree,* can be rendered easily by a simple drawing, but not its opposite (*The man does not plant a tree*). Whichever way one may try, this meaning cannot be communicated unambiguously and—depending on the graphic solution attempted—one arrives at inappropriate meanings like *A man beside a hole in the ground and an uprooted tree, Man and fallen tree,* or something of that kind. Experienced hypnotists therefore avoid negations and replace them, wherever possible, by positive formulations. To the patient who has just undergone surgery and is still under total anesthesia (and thus for all practical intents and purposes in a deep trance state), one would not try to suggest: "After awaking you will *not* feel nauseated" (which would not only violate the rule of the unresolved remnant—cf. page 73—but would be tantamount to a posthypnotic order to vomit), but rather: "About twenty minutes after returning to your room, you will feel, very much to your surprise, a pleasant sensation of appetite." Since appetite and nausea are mutually exclusive, the essential suggestion is thereby given and it is moreover implied that something pleasant will take place which for the patient (that is, his left-hemispheric reason) will be unexpected and incomprehensible.

Also this kind of intervention is by no means limited to hypnosis. Any injunction, any instruction is much more effective when given in positive language—that is, free from negation. "Remember to mail this letter" is bound to be remembered much more reliably, especially by a child, than "Don't forget to mail this letter."

In this connection, a brief remark on aversive formulations seems in order; that is, of formulations which in one way or another are directed against well-being, relaxation, and the like, and which—even though only indirectly—amount to negations. Instead of suggesting: "Cigarettes will taste horrible and you will have a terrible cough every time you smoke one," the incomparably more effective suggestion is: "In a few days [of not smoking] your respiration will be easy and smooth; the breathing of clear, clean air will produce a sense of well-being all through your body; and you will be proud of having freed yourself from your dependence on cigarettes through your own power." This, too, is not limited to hypnotherapy, but has general validity for all communication: The more negative and frightening a linguistic formulation, the less the other will be willing to accept it and the sooner he will forget it. Positive and concrete formulations are preconditions of any successful influence.

With this reference to concreteness I have already touched upon another subject: The *deliberate concretization* and consequent demolition of rhetorical abstractions.

"Private Katz," asks the sergeant (presumably in the old Prussian army), "why should the soldier gladly die for his emperor?" "Right you are; why should he?" replies Katz, and in doing so presumably blocks the sergeant's neurons for a while. For to *explain* what went awry here is by no means easy, and the victim is very likely to drop the issue. The *Gestapo*, however, did not drop the issue when one fine morning they found on propaganda posters with the pompous question, "National Socialism or Bolshevik chaos?" little stickers with the words: *"Erdäpfel oder Kartoffel?"* (spuds or potatoes?). And what remains of the rhetoric of the popular saying, "Where there is smoke, there must be fire," when the Viennese humorist Roda Roda adds: "But a pile of fresh manure will do just as well"?

I have already referred to the diabolical mastery of Karl Kraus' language. Here are two more examples from *Die Fackel*: "This is incomprehensible to those who value their professional honor so highly that it can no longer be perceived by the naked eye" and "Nothing is dearer to the military than their word of honor. But rebates are offered on purchase of larger quantities."

What these examples are meant to show is that rhetorical, bombastic, seemingly unquestionable statements can be demolished much better through concretization than through replies in the same language, no matter how precious and pretentious. And the way in which we may construct our world image, our "immutable," pain-producing reality, is only too often rhetorical, bombastic, and apparently unquestionable. The nonchalant remark, "The good old days have never existed," can be more therapeutic than a long, beastly serious interpretation of a person's infantile attitudes. The same goes for the suggestion: "Whoever thinks that they cannot live *without* a certain person, usually cannot live *with* him." Or remember Talleyrand's famous aphorism: "*On peut fair tout avec les baïonettes, sauf s'asseoir dessus*" (One can do anything with [the power of] bayonets, except to sit down on them)—for even the most powerful must sit down every once in a while. The Asian proverb: "He who rides the tiger cannot dismount," marvelously conveys through its first five words the image of total subjugation of bestial ferocity, while the next two drive home the practical impossibility and above all the precarious exposure of this heroic solution. Of course, only few people have the talent to find such subtle comparisons and *bon mots* in the heat of battle, but this does not rule out that as therapists we can train ourselves in the use of these speech patterns.

PARS PRO TOTO

It is in the nature of complex totalities that parts of them may, in a peculiar way, substitute *pro toto*—that is, for the whole. This was briefly mentioned already on page 22. The few lines of a caricature, the single bar of a symphony, the scent which brings back into consciousness a complex experience in its rich immediacy are examples of this phenomenon. Who has not had the experience of feeling immediately (and irrationally) attracted or repelled by a stranger simply because—as we usually realize much later—a minor physical or behavioral trait evoked within us the memory of another person?

The same illusionary mechanism is at work in representational art. Professor Ernst H. Gombrich of the University of London invites us to sketch an eyeless face and to watch the experience of relief when two dots at last enable it to look at us [49]. Admittedly, the eyes probably are the most important part of the totality of a face, the "mirror of the soul" (which is not only a poetic expression, but evidenced by their significance in symbolism and psychopathology). But as Gombrich's little experiment shows, even two casual dots can have this Gestalt-evoking quality and represent the visual incantation, so to speak, which changes the expression of an image or brings it to life in the first place. In this, I believe, lies the importance of Gombrich's observation for our subject matter. Richard Gombrich reports an even more pertinent example from Ceylon, where it is believed that the painting of the eyes of a Buddha statue, otherwise completed in all detail, finally brings the image to life:

The ceremony is regarded by its performers as very dangerous and is surrounded with tabus. . . . the craftsman paints in the eyes at an auspicious moment and is left alone in the closed temple with only his colleagues, while everyone else stands clear even of the outer door. Moreover, the craftsman does not dare to look the statue in the face, but keeps his back to it and paints sideways or over his shoulder while looking into a mirror, which catches the gaze of the image he is bringing to life. As soon as the painting is done, the craftsman himself has a dangerous gaze. [50]

The conclusion to be drawn from this for the technique of therapeutic discourse is that the *pars-pro-toto* principle is another vehicle that seems to bypass the left half of the brain and to permit direct communication with the right half. Of course, this intervention also presupposes not only a degree of creative fantasy, but presence of mind. Yet the ability to empathize with a client's world image is, after all, a precondition of successful therapy. *Pars-pro-toto* communication is particularly indicated where, for whatever reasons (for example, strangeness, enormity, apparent senselessness) the perception of a complex totality is difficult. If somebody were to try to explain the ferocious violence of a tornado, he would tend to describe how entire roofs, buses, or uprooted trees are being hurled through the air. This sounds impressive, but can hardly be imagined. If, however, he mentions that he saw a heavy wooden door into which a straw had embedded itself like a nail, we suddenly have an approximate measure for the otherwise unimaginable fury of the storm: the straw, epitomy of thinness and fragility, hit the door with such force that it did not have the time to splinter before it had already been driven deeply into the wood. This image conveys a far more immediate impression than a long description of the path of destruction running straight through a town.

Perhaps we must include in the *pars-pro-toto* phenomena those not at all infrequent, bizarre acts of desperation triggered by some trivial misfortune: the train, missed by a few seconds; a lost handkerchief; the broken shoelace.* Allegorically one then talks about the straw that broke the camel's back. Literally, however, it may indeed be the sudden *pars-pro-toto* awareness· of a deep unhappiness or hopelessness whose actual extent we may be able to ignore until it reveals itself, suddenly and unbearably, in the realm of the trivial.

* Cf. the following excerpt from Charles Bukowski's poem "The Shoelace":

. . . It's not the large things that
send a man to the
madhouse, . . .
No, it's the continuing series of small tragedies
that send a man to the madhouse . . .
not the death of his love
but a shoelace that snaps
with no time left . . .

Here, too, the principle *similia similibus curantur* holds true. Many therapies appear to fail or to drag on indefinitely because of the constant, utopian attempt to deal with The Problem in all its supposed depth and ramifications. The armamentarium of hypnotherapy, on the other hand, contains interventions that are compatible with system-oriented (and not only individual) psychotherapy and that have shown their power and effectiveness as minimal, but goal-specific techniques in brief therapy. Admittedly, compared to the apparent sophistication of the traditional past-oriented, intrapsychic approach, the directness and simplicity of their *pars-pro-toto* nature makes them appear superficial and mechanistic. Often it is the patients themselves who reject a small, concrete change, precisely because it seems to overlook the "real" problem. Not infrequently, this attitude is reinforced by the widespread conviction that "real" therapy must be long and consist chiefly of explanations. Even under the best of circumstances, the decisive step from mere talking to doing—that is, actively intervening in order to change a concrete situation— is very difficult. But if this step can be induced, and if the intervention leads to the change of a seemingly trivial aspect of the all-embracing problem, it then often becomes apparent that, after all, the problem was not as monolithic as it seemed. On the other hand, the patient may be willing to accept the *pars* precisely because of its apparent insignificance in comparison to the *totum*, and this may especially be the case if the therapist avails himself of those means of therapeutic influence which I have presented elsewhere [117] and which shall be further exemplified in the following chapters.

For the time being, let me merely suggest that the effect of a successful *pars-pro-toto* intervention most probably does not simply lie in the fact that—in the traditional sense—the right interpretation is given at the right moment (that is, when the patient is ready to admit the repressed into consciousness and thus arrives at insight). Rather, the essence of the intervention is most probably due to the power of the *pars* not only to represent the *totum*, but to restructure it and thereby to modify a world image. But to bring about such a change knowingly and willingly (instead of attributing it to intuition, insight, or chance) requires the knowledge of the world image that is to be changed. This necessity will occupy us again in the section on *reframing*.

There is yet another aspect of the *pars-pro-toto* principle which, strictly speaking, is not directly related to the subject at hand, but which may conveniently be included here. It is the basic hypnotherapeutic rule of the *unresolved remnant*, which is just as valid for general psychotherapy. In essence this rule states that one should never aim at the complete, total solution of a problem, but only at its improvement or lessening; for instance, that the patient will feel *less* pain, or that he will sleep *a little* longer, or that he will probably always experience a measure of discomfort in an elevator, but that it will be tolerable. The effect of leaving an unresolved remnant is twofold: It lifts the whole idea of change out of the all-or-none utopia of either complete success or total failure, and it enables the patient to go, on his own, well beyond the change that the therapist seems to consider possible. The patient thus leaves treatment with a much greater confidence in his own capabilities and much less dependence on the crutches of therapy.

APHORISMS

According to Webster, an aphorism is "a short, pointed sentence expressing a wise or clever observation or a general truth." In it at least two concepts or thoughts are brought into an association that is unusual, startling, and therefore (or perhaps in spite of its seemingly contradictoriness) has an immediate impact. When Hölderlin, for instance, explains that "what has made the State into hell is that man wanted to make it into his heaven," he plays with an unusual juxtaposition of *heaven* and *hell*. The same goes for the expression, "Too little to live on, too much to starve from," for normally we associate *dying* with *too little*. But not only do we not protest the logical absurdity of this dictum (after all, there is no third possibility besides life or death) but, again, these ten words convey a much more immediate, palpable sense than an explanation that respects the laws of logic and reason. It seems that there is something in the essence of a well-constructed aphorism that lends itself to an almost flashlike illumination of complex human situations and, therefore, also of world images. When the Hungarian poet Gyula Sipos concludes his poem, "If it is not worth it," with the lines, ". . . if there is nothing worth dying for, life, too, is worth nothing," he highlights the interdependence of the meaning of life and death much more clearly and immediately than a more philosophical explanation could possible achieve with twice as many words.

A particularly effective form of aphorism is the so-called *chiasm*. This is a language pattern of crosslike structure that owes its name to the Greek letter *chi* (**X**). Kopperschmidt analyzes form and content of the chiasm by using the following description of the bourgeois society contained in the *Communist Manifesto* (1848):

. . . for those who work do not acquire anything, and those who acquire anything do not work. . . .

and he goes on to explain:

. . .The above-mentioned lexical elements form two syntactic sequences (sub-clauses) of eight elements each, whose equivalence is

74

further intensified by the lexical identity . . . of their syntactic members. This so-called syntactic and lexical *parallelism* would lead to formal triviality and tautology of content, if at one point of this parallelism there did not occur a lexical break, turning the principle of repetition into a contrasting pattern. . . . The chiastic association of the lexically corresponding members further amounts to a semantic juxtaposition within the statement and the reversal of its meaning. . . . [72, p. 166]

The basic pattern of this chiasm is thus:

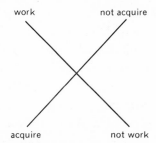

This perplexing structure through which a complex state of affairs is apparently reduced to utter simplicity and clarity, and which belongs much more to our right- than our left-hemispheric "syntax," probably accounts for the electrifying effect of a chiasm. Small wonder that it is dear to the hearts of politicians, demagogues, and marketing experts. When in 1809 Ferdinand Schill addressed his anti-Napoleonic volunteer corps with the words that since then have become proverbial:

* "Rather an end with (that is, full of) terror, than terror without end!"

the situation seemed completely clarified, the right decision un-questionable, and the last doubt removed that besides these alter-natives there could possibly be other solutions. The situation as such (that is, its first-order reality) was still the same, but what was changed was the *view* that those concerned had of it. In this capacity to influence second-order realities lies the power of chiastic communications and their usefulness for the modifica-tion of world images—again, of course, in a good as well as in a bad sense. A practical example would be the remark which ob-tains for a number of problem situations: "The tenser you be-come, the more you pull yourself together; and the more you pull yourself together, the tenser you become," even though it lacks the structural rigor of the preceding examples. But even so it con-denses the complex structure of a vicious circle into a concise, easily understandable formula. And when Oscar Wilde aphorizes sarcastically: "The only difference between a saint and a sinner is that every saint has a past and every sinner has a future," he demolishes the terrible simplification of a typical black-and-white painting of human nature; just as, regrettably, the *bon mot*: "Foreign aid consists in taking money away from the poor people in rich countries and giving it to the rich people in poor coun-tries," hits the nail right on the head. When a certain brand of transparent wrapping material is advertised with the chiastic slogan:

Protects what it shows,

shows what it protects

very little factual information is given, but an impression of special significance is created. When, all contrary reasons and factual evidence notwithstanding, the politically powerful National Rifle Association justifies its resistance to any legal limitations on the free possession and sale of firearms with the slogan:

If guns are outlawed,

only outlaws will have guns

we are faced with the pseudologic (and its behavioral effects) of a chiasm that is bound to sound convincing, especially to the less responsible elements of society.

Chiasms also form the basis of many forms of humor. Freud quotes Spitzer, who in his *Wiener Spaziergänge* [Viennese Walks] tells the following joke:

Mr. and Mrs. X live in fairly grand style. Some people think that the husband has earned a lot and so has been able to lay by a bit [*sich etwas zurückgelegt*]; others again think that the wife has lain back a bit [*sich etwas zurückgelegt*] and so has been able to earn a lot. [109]

And Freud adds admiringly: "A really diabolically ingenious joke!" [38, p. 33].

AMBIGUITIES, PUNS, ALLUSIONS

This joke leads us into the wide field of *ambiguities, puns, allusions*, and the like, whose rich flora is difficult to classify. *Sich etwas zurückgelegt* is first used in a figurative, metaphorical, and a moment later in its concrete, physical sense, and out of this sleight-of-hand arises the barb. Words that are spelled and pronounced alike but have different meanings are said to be *homonymous*, and Shakespeare (and his contemporaries) were already fond of their semantic potential. In *The Two Gentlemen of Verona* (I, 2), for instance, Lucetta drops a letter by Proteus, but quickly picks it up again and thereby awakens Julia's curiosity:

Julia: And is this paper nothing?
Lucetta: Nothing concerning me.
Julia: Then let it lie for those that it concerns.
Lucetta: Madam, it will not lie where it concerns.

The two meanings of "lie" in this example are truly homonymous, since both their spelling and pronunciation are identical. But even where this is not quite the case, as in many puns, the immediacy of the effect is not necessarily diminished, but may often be enhanced through the additional element of condensation. *Circus viscosus* instead of *circulus vitiosus*, or *Don Coyote* instead of *Don Quixote* have all the qualities of a slip of the tongue, but may just as well be very clever, deliberate formulations. Several years ago a newly appointed Secretary of Labor in the Franco regime issued an order that all government employees in Spain had to start work at 9 o'clock in the morning. At about the same time the first reports of the alleged Yeti, the abominable snow man of the Himalayas (in Spanish: *el abominable hombre de la nieve*), reached the West. This earned the minister the title: *El abominable hombre de las nueve* (the abominable 9 o'clock man).

Right-Hemispheric Language Patterns

The deliberate utilization of homonyms, with their inherent ambiguities and absurdities, can play a powerful role in therapeutic communication and has always played this role in hypnotherapy. Its effect appears to lie in circumventing or blocking the logical, critical censorship of the left hemisphere by the use of phonetically identical (homophonic), but semantically distinct words out of which the right hemisphere can then choose the meaning that appears relevant or appropriate. *Right, write,* and *rite* sound identical, but have very distinct meanings, and English, more than most Indo-European languages, abounds in homonyms and homophones.* Erickson, for instance will use *a part* and *apart* when he wants to suggest the idea that something that in his client's view is *a part* of the problem may now no longer belong to the problem and, therefore, turn out to be *apart*. Or Erickson may juggle with the semantic ambiguity of *certain*, which, depending on the context, may either mean *sure, expectable,* or almost the opposite—that is, *indefinite* or even *unknown* (as in: "a certain Brown called and left a message" or "there is a certain confusion"). Needless to say, also with this type of intervention the limits are set by the therapist's inventiveness and linguistic sophistication.

Also the opposite is possible: *Synonyms*, that is, different words with the same meaning, may become the agents of change where the ingredients of a situation appear unchangeable. A prime example is the maxim: *"Se obedece pero no se cumple"* ("One obeys but does not comply"), which enabled the officers of the Spanish Crown in the Central American possessions to cope with the imperial orders from Madrid. The trouble with these orders was that very often they could not be obeyed because they were the results

---

* French is a close runner-up to English. Among many other examples, Gauger [43] mentions that Voltaire used to annoy Frederick the Great by pointing out to him that the name of his summer residence, *Sans Souci*, did not only mean (literally) "without sorrow" or "without sorrows," but also "a hundred sorrows" (*cent soucis*).

of the Escorial's abysmal ignorance of the actual state of affairs in the overseas territories, or because by the time they arrived they were hopelessly obsolete as a result of further developments in the meantime. Both *obedecer* and *cumplir* mean *to obey, to carry out an instruction*. What then was the practical meaning of the advice to do the one but not the other? But it is just this synonymity of the two verbs that suggests that two different things must be meant by their apparently redundant juxtaposition; namely that on the one hand one does not disobey, but that on the other hand one does not carry out the instruction either. In other words: One does what the *real* situation requires, but one does it within the frame of apparent compliance with an unrealistic order.

A special case, usually combining some of the elements mentioned in the foregoing, is the *euphemism*. It consists, to quote Webster again, in "the substitution of an agreeable or inoffensive expression for one that may offend or suggest something unpleasant." For the student of therapeutic communication, however, it might be more to the point to define it as yet another species of messages by which realities may be created—or distorted, depending on one's semantic preference. We are seldom aware of the barrage of these prettifying word games with which culture, tradition, propaganda, and the advertising industry bombard us incessantly. Old people do not prosaically die, rather "senior citizens" eventually "pass on." Garbage collectors have been promoted to the dignity of "sanitation workers"; promiscuity may result in a "social disease" or a "love child"; the homosexual is "a woman trapped in the body of a man"; the unemployment office has become the "employment development department"; War Departments have coyly been replaced by Defense Departments, the dirty word itself surviving only in the righteous concept of "war of liberation"; and we even have a "clean bomb." Only occasionally is this sugary language turned upside down—for example, when some jester refers to "love" and "work" as four-letter words.

No doubt, in accordance with Vance Packard, the advertising industry must be credited with having promoted to a high degree of perfection the irrational persuasiveness hidden in euphemisms, especially when they are enriched with alliterations, mere clang associations, deliberately induced moot conclusions ("milk from contented cows"), pseudoexplanations ("I smoke for pleasure," therefore my smoking is not an addiction), meaningless superlatives (there are three types of wool material in Italy: *lana* (wool), *pura* (pure) lana, and *purissima lana*—the last, therefore, being purer than pure and thus just plain wool), deliberate semantic contaminations ("genuine imported polyester"— what on earth would imitation polyester be and what difference does it make that it is imported?), and many other semantic stultifications.

Occasionally one must grudgingly admire their cleverness; for instance, when *Campari* is advertised with the slogan: "There Is No Camparison!" A truly sophisticated example, combining digital and analogic elements, is the advertisement shown on page 82. The literal meaning of *"Cada vez me gusta más"* is "Each time I like . . . better." Because of the missing personal pronoun, this is an incomplete sentence in English, but it is not in Spanish, where the statement is syntactically and semantically well-formed, although undecidable: it remains unclear *whom* or *what* the young lady likes better each time. It is in this ambiguity that the clever effect of the advertisement resides. My friend and colleague Verón, to whom I owe this example, has subjected it to a detailed analysis whose salient points I want to summarize here: The picture shows a man in the process of getting dressed. (The position of his hands leaves no doubt that he is dressing; nobody would or could take his tie *off* that way.) But dressing implies a

(cada vez me gusta más)

CAMISAS
VAN HEUSEN

preceding state of nakedness which, in turn, is given a sexual connotation by the presence of the girl and is reinforced by her dreamy look. The focused clarity of his face, contrasted by the transparency of hers, sets further accents: He represents the con-

82

crete, real world; of him it is implied that his masculine, demanding sex appeal gets him what he wants, while she is dreaming with open eyes. And of what? Not only of this one time, but of *cada vez*—of every past and, therefore, also every future time, of which she likes every new time better than the preceding one. Thus we are informed by the five words in parentheses, which obviously express her thought. But as a result of the missing personal pronoun, these words can have three different meanings which fuse together into a vague, but suggestive impression: Every time she likes *him*, *her* (the shirt [*camisa*], which in Spanish is of feminine gender) or *it* (lovemaking) better. "And since these semantic alternatives in their indeterminacy are equally present," writes Verón, "this enchanted shirt represents a delicate epitome of sex, the love of beautiful women, success and presumably many other such things" [112]. And, I am inclined to add, although this shirt is still a prosaic shirt, its significance in the world image of the beholder of this advertisement, its second-order reality, is markedly changed.*

When we utilize such Gestalt-creating ambiguities we need not worry too much about digital logic. Not rarely is it the actual or apparent absurdity of such formulations that makes them especially convincing. "*Soyez réalistes, demandez l'impossible*" (Be realistic, demand the impossible) was scrawled on many houses during the riots in Paris in 1968, expressing very concisely that,

---

* The similarity between advertising and political propaganda is obvious. But there is at least one difference in favor of consumerism, and it is, to quote Schneider once more:

. . . a decisive difference that is rarely taken into account: Even in its excesses advertising is more humane, more tolerant, more liberal than propaganda—namely in its effect, and this is what matters. Very much in contrast to political persuasion, commercial manipulation does not want to furnish us a closed world image, at worst it changes us *half-way*. And in contrast to propaganda it is not *dangerous* to shun it. It is certainly difficult: To choose in the din of the detergent manufacturers' drum roll the most reasonable product or to reject them all in favor of just plain soap—this is quite beyond many people. But those who succeed are neither arrested nor outlawed. [98, p. 152]

as the students saw the political situation, only a change that was total but therefore impossible within the existing political framework would be realistic.*

Ambiguity can be pushed further. There is a suggestive, evocative power in what at first blush may seem a jumble of words, violating the rules of grammar and syntax—for instance, a description of poor, barren western Mexico, containing the sentence: ". . . not fat fat green chile relleno red jacaranda blossom mariachi band caballero sombrero Tourist Mexico . . ." [122]. Also these language forms have their definite place in the armamentarium of hypnotherapy. Compare this example with the structure of a brief quotation from a trance induction that Erickson used with a terminal cancer patient called Joe. A tumor had been removed from Joe's face; he was in great pain and could not speak. He had spent his life as a gardener, and Erickson decided to utilize this "language" and to intersperse it with pain-relieving suggestions. For greater clarity, these suggestions are italicized:

. . . I wonder if the tomato plant can, *Joe, feel really feel a kind of comfort*. You know, Joe, a plant is a wonder thing, and *it is so nice, so pleasing* just to be able to think about a plant as if it were a man. Would such a plant *have nice feelings, a sense of comfort* as the tiny little tomatoes begin to form, so tiny, yet so *full of promise to give you the desire to eat* a luscious tomato, sun-ripened, it's so *nice to have food in one's stomach*, that wonderful feeling a child, a thirsty child, has and *can want a drink*, Joe, is that the way the tomato plant feels when the rain falls and washes everything so that *all feels well* (pause). . . . [29]

While the left hemisphere may stumble over the constant switches of referents, the grammatical inconsistencies and the general confusion of these sentences, the right hemisphere processes the interspersed suggestions. Bandler and Grinder [3, pp.

---

* The slogan has a suspicious similarity with Tertullian's proposition: *"Certum est quia impossibile est"* (It is certain, because it is impossible; *De Carne Christi*, chapter 5), which is usually quoted incorrectly but not nonsensically as *"Credo quia absurdum est"* (I believe, because it is absurd).

233–40] have presented in greater detail the use of ambiguities by Erickson. He may, for instance, create a trance-inducing ambiguity by condensing two injunctions into the "ungrammatical" sentence: "I want you to notice your hand me the glass."

Much better known than these phonetic-semantic ambiguities, and therefore much more readily available as an aid in the split-second decisions that crucial therapy situations often require, are those allusions, insinuations, and innuendos that are part and parcel of everyday language. Here too, of course, we find every shade and degree of mastery. When the Viennese actor Girardi wrote to the author of a particularly negative critique: "I am sitting in the smallest room of my flat; your review of last night's performance still *before* me," he implied something that, expressed less ambiguously, would have been rather vulgar. Or consider the rich implications condensed into one short sentence from a case description by Selvini: "He had married her more or less out of gratitude for having cured him of impotence" [103]. "Man without a woman is like a fish without a bicycle" would be yet another, although hardly therapeutic, example, and so is the witticism: Statistics are like a bikini; what they reveal is suggestive, what they conceal is vital.

There exist, then, certain language forms that enable us to say something without quite saying it. Let us look at their structure by means of two further examples. The first is the cartoon be-

BORN LOSER   **by Art Sansom**

low. It gives the starting and the ending point of a somewhat involved train of thought which, however, is itself missing. In other words, the result is there in its final form and has a definite and immediate impact, but to understand what exactly it means and how we got there, we have to reconstruct that train of reasoning which runs underground, so to speak. This now is the task of the left hemisphere, and it looks somewhat like this:

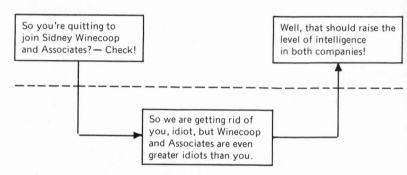

The other example is the old story, quoted also by Freud [38, pp. 68–69], of the king who, while traveling through a village, noticed a man in the crowd who bore a striking resemblance to his own exalted person. He beckoned to him and asked: "Was your mother at one time in service in the Palace?" "No, your Highness," was the reply, "but my father was."

In this example, too, the impact of the crucial piece of information is much more powerful and immediate than that of a more "typical," "open" way of formulating the same response, but on the other hand, it leaves its offensive element unsaid yet clearly implied. In other words: There seems to be a tacit rule of communication that what is said without being said is not "really" said, but somehow is communicated with particular power.* The same is, of course, true of every joke. Its point is lost

---

* In this connection cf. also the section on preempting (pp. 150–53).

if one has to explain it—that is, translate it into the language of the left hemisphere and its poor sense of humor.

In this mechanism lies the therapeutic potential of this type of communication. To be sure, in therapy there is no need to offend, but very often there is a need to bring out into the open some element of which it may be safely assumed that it will be painful, embarrassing or otherwise unacceptable to the client. "How much of a problem is alcohol for you?" is a much more tactful and tactical question than, "How much do you drink?" The former question sounds neutral, it insinuates nothing and thus bypasses the client's defenses rather than to meet them head-on. But at the same time it implies not only the possibility, but even the likelihood that he does drink. By the same token, therapists ought to be aware of the ever-present danger of unintended negative implications in therapeutic discourse. This problem arises only too easily, especially when the client is either oversensitive in a certain area or when for some other reason he is already inclined to see things in a certain way. The seemingly innocent remark by a therapist during an initial interview in January, "By the way, in August I always take my vacation," is likely to drive home even to the more optimistic patients that the treatment will be long. Under the same rubric come the linguistic sins of many doctors who—whether through pessimism or through apodictic forecasts or other predictions—negatively influence the course of an illness in an almost posthypnotic way.

Fortunately, the same mechanism lends itself equally to positive forms of influence. Examples are: "Try to overeat just enough so that you will lose between three and four pounds per week" or (as posthypnotic suggestion) "As a result of your self-hypnosis, eating will become for you a pleasure the like of which you have never experienced before. The *smallest quantity of food will taste so much better* and ful*fill* (homophony will *fill*, satiate, but also with "fulfilling your wish to lose weight") you so much more than large meals did ever *before* (both the grammatically incorrect past tense and the stress on *before* imply that the problem already belongs to the past)." In both these examples, the left hemisphere is likely to be blocked by the logical nonsense of the messages (*Overeat* to lose weight? Enjoy eating even *more*?) while the right hemisphere, with its very different, archaic logic literally "gets the message." Or consider the absurd formulation: "Your problem will probably bother you for quite some time to come—maybe even three or four weeks," which is much more effective than the equivalent, logical, confident formulation which seems to be called for when there is reason to believe that change is now possible but still requires a gentle push. On the other hand, the remark: "Oh, I agree, your improvement will probably come very unexpectedly," made in response to the patient's disappointment or impatience with the course of therapy, can create a therapeutically very desirable confusion through the way in which it contradicts his pessimism. Without directly saying so, it insinuates agreement where the patient disagrees and thereby implies that his discontent is unrealistic. Somewhat the same effect is achieved by the turned-around aphorism: The situation is hopeless but not serious.

The use of innuendos—the art of not saying something in order to say it—is, of course, by no means a discovery of interactional psychotherapy, but has always played an important role in diplomacy (defined by somebody as the art of getting others to do by their *own* decision what you want them to do) and in comparable social contexts. Here is one more example, this one from literature, highlighting the essence of this form of communication. In Hugo von Hofmannsthal's comedy *The Difficult Man,* the young Crescence inquires about one of the guests from her host, Count Altenwyl:

Right-Hemispheric Language Patterns

Crescence: I met an entirely new face at my bridge-table, and Mariette Stradonitz whispered to me that he's a world-famous scholar we've never heard of simply because we're all illiterate.

Altenwyl: Professor Brücke is a great celebrity in his subject and a welcome political colleague of mine. He enjoys enormously being in a drawing-room where he meets with no colleagues from the academic world, so that he is, as it were, the sole representative of learning in a purely social circle, and since my house can offer him this modest indulgence—

Crescence: Is he married?

Altenwyl: At any rate I have never had the honour of meeting Madame Brücke.

Crescence: I find famous men odious, but their wives are still worse. Kari agrees with me there. We're all for trivial people and trivial conversations, aren't we, Kari?

Altenwyl: I have my own old-fashioned predilections, Helen knows what they are.

Crescence: You should back me up, Kari. I find that nine-tenths of what passes for intellectual conversation is just twaddle. [56]

And thus the conversation goes on, with Altenwyl saying much without saying much, and nobody could pin him down to any one of his statements.

In order to put some structure into the inevitable hodge-podge of the many shadings and nuances of the language forms mentioned in this chapter, it might be useful to quote here from an article by Muir, dealing with the properties of the "serious pun" in Shakespeare's work—properties that are common to most of the examples given above:

There are four main functions of the serious pun in dramatic poetry. First, puns—and especially hidden puns—provide . . . an illogical reinforcement of the logical sequence of thought, so that the poetic statement strikes us almost as a remembrance—as Keats said that poetry should do. Secondly, such puns often link together unrelated imagery and act as solvents for mixed metaphors. Thirdly, they make the listener aware of a complex of ideas which enrich the total statement, even though they do not come into full consciousness. Fourthly, they seem to shoot out roots in all directions, so that the poetry is firmly based on reality—a reality which is nothing less, if nothing more, than the sum total of experience. [80]

To conclude this chapter: There are certain linguistic patterns which the present state of our knowledge permits us to call right-hemispheric and which are, therefore, particularly conducive to therapeutic communication. While it is impossible to order them into something like a therapy manual—which would necessitate for every single example a long anamnestic description of the context—the study of their appearance in everyday language, especially when coupled with a knowledge of their function in hypnosis, can lead to increasing mastery in their utilization. This chapter was, therefore, devoted to the presentation of these patterns by means of examples from many different areas of language use.

7

Blocking

the Left Hemisphere

THERE EXISTS another method of gaining access to the right hemisphere, and it is fundamentally different from, but not incompatible with, the approach described in the preceding chapter. It consists in blocking or circumventing the left hemisphere and thereby permitting the right to become dominant—a technique which, it may be assumed, virtually amounts to a functional commissurotomy.

As mentioned on page 36, this temporary, functional antagonism between the two halves of the brain may be present in psychosomatic conditions; it is probably also involved in dissociative states and may account for the clinically well known primary-process manifestations.

Much less is known about those frames of mind that arise spontaneously in life-threatening situations and similar moments of crisis. In contrast to psychopathological states, they distinguish themselves by an unusual degree of reality adaptation, instantaneous evaluation of the situation, and maximally appropriate, rapid action. Subjectively, these states are experienced as an almost complete absence of panic, helplessness, or confusion—so much so that afterwards one is amazed to realize that in a fraction of a second and without time to think one managed to take the most appropriate course of action. Aldous Huxley quotes from the report of a young psychiatrist who served during World War II as a medical observer with the Eighth Air Force in England:

He went on one mission, during which the B-17 plane and crew were so severely damaged that survival seemed impossible. He had already studied the "on the ground" personalities of the crew and had found that they represented a great diversity of human types. Of their behavior in crisis he reported:

"Their reactions were remarkably alike. During the violent combat and in the acute emergencies that arose during it, they were all quietly precise on the interphone and decisive in action. The tail gunner, right waist gunner and nagivator were severely wounded early in the fight, but all three kept at their duties efficiently and without cessation. The burden of emergency work fell on the pilot, engineer and ball turret gunner, and all functioned with rapidity, skillful effectiveness and no lost motion. The burden of the decisions, during, but particularly after the combat, rested essentially on the pilot and, in secondary details, on the co-pilot and bombardier. The decisions, arrived at with care and speed, were unquestioned once they were made, and proved excellent. In the period when disaster was momentarily expected, the alternative plans of action were made clearly and with no thought other than the safety of the entire crew. All at this point were quiet, unobtrusively cheerful and ready for anything. There was at no time paralysis, panic, unclear thinking, faulty or confused judgment, or self-seeking in any one of them.

One could not possibly have inferred from their behaviour that this one was a man of unstable moods and that that one was a shy, quiet, introspective man. They all became outwardly calm, precise in thought and rapid in action." [60]

Blocking the Left Hemisphere

Perhaps even more interesting is a recent study carried out by two researchers at the University of Iowa. They interviewed 70 men and 34 women who had survived extremely life-threatening situations. About half the cases involved mountain climbing accidents; the others included near-drownings, battlefield experiences, and physical emergencies like cardiac arrests or severe allergic reactions. Almost all the subjects reported a slowing of "external time," a feeling of calmness and of freedom from anxiety, but especially the experience of an almost filmlike, endless stream of vivid images of past events that came to their minds' eye in a freshness and immediacy as if they were taking place at that very moment. [81].

The question of whether these states are due to the right hemisphere suddenly becoming dominant or, rather, to an unusually high integration of interhemispheric functioning probably cannot be answered at the present state of our knowledge. What is striking, however, is that two predominantly right-hemispheric phenomena are involved: the peculiar timelessness of those brief seconds and the visual reexperience of large parts of one's life, almost as if in a film.

It goes without saying that such life-endangering crisis situations cannot be deliberately engineered in order to gain access to these areas of one's inner world. Hallucinogenic drugs seem to have comparable effects, but most of their users find it difficult, if not impossible, to bring back anything useful from "over there" into their everyday lives.

However, in therapy we do have some less drastic methods for the temporary blocking of reason's critical-analytic, logical censorship. Above all, Erickson's *confusion technique* [27] must be mentioned in this connection. It is particularly indicated with people who tend to intellectualize and to talk everything to pieces. As the term implies, this method is essentially a way of

93

producing a state of intellectual confusion, be it by means of extremely complex, pseudological explanations, be it through very ponderous, complicated, and therefore confusing references to the most trivial facts, or by a combination of both. Modeled after Erickson, and in practice, of course, much more drawn out and monotonous, a confusion might be initiated in the following way:

One thinks and thinks and things are relative my thoughts to yours and yours to mine and my chair is here and your chair for me is there because my here is here and my there is there and for you my there is your here and your there is here for me just as in time because the same time is the present but your eighteenth birthday came before your nineteenth but the seventeenth was in the past and the eighteenth was now and now you think of the future in which the future became the present of your twentieth birthday and what birthday present you may have been getting to go is easy you can do it just as you can do it with the meaning of words is that some of them have their own meaning and others do not have their own meaning because the word *short* is itself short but the word *long* is not itself long in fact it is shorter than short and the word *español* is Spanish but the word Spanish is not Spanish it is English and as you think of it you know that you have always known this and did not think it. . . .

Into this stream of inanities and obscurities the actual suggestions are then either interspersed, as mentioned on page 60, and thus made inaccessible to intellectualizations, or they are given suddenly and clearly in the midst of this intellectual fog as the only concrete piece of meaning which is, therefore, grasped and held onto with particular tenacity. But the above example should not give the impression that the confusion technique can be used only in hypnosis. It is mentioned here precisely because it can be taken over into general therapeutic communication, although here the confusion-producing pseudologic must be a little more sophisticated. But who has not yet had the experience of trying in vain to follow a complicated and confusing explanation and eventually holding on only to the concrete, understandable conclusion? The result is thus virtually the same.* In a similar vein, Erickson will ask a question of a subject who tends to use intellectualizations and verbalizations as a way of resisting, and then, just as the other is about to answer, ask him another question and then yet another. The patient is thus forced into constant mental shifts without ever being allowed to bring his thought processes to a conclusion by verbalizing an answer. The result is an intellectual blockage.

This method is not limited to hypnotherapy, and not even to the therapeutic dialogue, but can even be used monologically, so to speak, by insomniacs. Who has not experienced, in his own sleepless hours, that seemingly inescapable treadmill of his thoughts, about which also our patients with sleep disorders complain almost without exception? If it were only possible to stop these thoughts from running around in vicious circles, then— they surmise, not without justification—sleep would probably come. They usually agree that their thoughts are a monologue or an imaginary dialogue which, just like any other spoken sentence, follow the laws of grammar and syntax. But just as it is perfectly possible for a speaker to interrupt himself and not to complete his sentence, one can also interrupt one's thoughts and refuse to think them to their grammatical conclusion. It is possi-

* The exact opposite of the confusion technique also constitutes an effective intervention. It obtains in situations in which as a result of panic or great pain somebody already *is* in a state that amounts to confusion. Here the hypnotherapeutic technique of shifting attention may be very effective, except that in these cases the desired shift is from irrationality to rationality. The absurd question: "What did you have for breakfast this morning?" or "From what high school did you graduate?", followed by further, apparently related questions, all asked with an insistence and urgency of voice as if they were of the greatest immediate importance, may, precisely on account of their startling and incomprehensible lack of rhyme or reason, bring about the desired shift of attention away from the panic of the present situation.

ble to have the patient practice this in the therapy session and he will readily notice how every interrupted thought is immediately replaced by a new one which he again must interrupt and which is followed by a third one, and so on in seemingly endless succession. He is then told to practice this before falling asleep. Almost invariably he finds out that when he maintains this exercise for a very few minutes (which admittedly seem like hours) there arises a sleep-promoting intellectual confusion which leads from the logical, directed thinking of wakefulness into the imagery of dreaming. Depending on his world image the reader will probably see in this technique a warmed-over, modernized version of the age-old expedient of "counting sheep," or an application of the concept of *Buddhistic attention* which strives towards a maximal awareness of even our most routine thoughts, feelings, and actions as a way of liberation from the bonds of everyday life.

And this leads over to a subject whose detailed treatment would by far exceed the subject matter of this book, but which should be mentioned at least briefly. Mystics have always relied on certain exercises and mental techniques in order to free themselves from the illusion of the so-called reality. One such method is the Zen-Buddhistic *koan*, a mental exercise whose absurdity or paradoxical nature blocks the faculty of rational comprehension and thereby makes it fail. What then enters into consciousness is an awareness of one's world image precisely as *an image* of reality and not reality *itself*. Indeed, there is reason to assume that the so-called mystical experience occurs when—for whatever momentary reason—we manage to leave the curved space of the self-reflexiveness of our world image and for a fleeting moment succeed in seeing it "from the outside" and thus in its relativity. He who has experienced it knows that this is not a terrifying moment of disintegration and dissolution of reality, but rather conveys a sense of liberation and of ultimate existential security.

Blocking the Left Hemisphere

But to return from the esoteric to the purely technical aspects of practical therapy, let me repeat that the interventions described in this chapter are essentially based on an overload of the left hemisphere, which in turn permits direct communication with the right half of the brain. The comparison with a pick-pocket or a magician's trick cannot be entirely dismissed, since a deflection of attention away from the decisive action is indeed involved. The patient tries to follow the therapist's pseudologic and to resolve the paradox, but fails, while the right hemisphere has a chance to process those elements of the therapeutic communication that are understandable in its "language," and it thus becomes temporarily dominant.

In his story, *Mario and the Magician*, Thomas Mann describes the use of paradoxical language by a stage hypnotist. I am using this example here because, even though fictitious, a real hypnotist could have used precisely this language—in fact, one almost suspects that Mann took these inductions down in shorthand. The hypnotist, Cavaliere Cipolla, a rather unsavory individual who at the end of his performance falls victim to his own overbearing and degrading behavior, chooses as his first victim a heckler who made the audience laugh:

"Ah, bravo!" answered Cipolla. "I like you *giovanotto*. Trust me, I've had my eye on you for some time. People like you are just in my line. I can use them. And you are the pick of the lot, that's plain to see. *You do what you like. Or is it possible you have ever not done what you liked—or even, maybe, what you didn't like? What somebody else liked, in short?* Hark ye, my friend, that might be a pleasant change for you, to divide up the willing and the doing and stop tackling both jobs at once. Division of labor, *sistema americano, sai!* For instance, suppose you were to show your tongue to this select and honourable audience here—your whole tongue, right down to the roots?"

"No, I won't," said the youth, hostilely. "Sticking out your tongue shows a bad bringing-up."

"Nothing of the sort," retorted Cipolla. "You would only be *doing* it."

And then Cipolla counts to ten and, indeed, the youth sticks out his tongue as far as it will go. Later he suggests a colic to the same lad:

"My son, you do not feel much like joking," he said. "It is only too natural, for anyone can see that you are not feeling too well. Even your tongue, which leaves something to be desired on the score of cleanliness, indicates acute disorder of the gastric system. An evening entertainment is no place for people in your state; you yourself, I can tell, were of several minds whether you would not do better to put on a flannel bandage and go to bed. It was not good judgment to drink so much of that very sour white wine this afternoon. Now you have such a colic you would like to double up with the pain. Go ahead, don't be embarrassed. There is a distinct relief that comes from bending over, in cases of intestinal cramp. . . ."

"Double over," repeated Cipolla. "What else can you do? With a colic like that you *must* bend. *Surely you will not struggle against the performance of a perfectly natural action just because somebody suggests it to you?*"

And to another subject who lets him know that he is determined to assert his own will when drawing a card, Cipolla says:

"You will make my task somewhat more difficult thereby. As for the result, your resistance will not alter it in the least. *Freedom exists, and also the will exists; but freedom of the will does not exist, for a will that aims at its own freedom aims at the unknown.* You are free to draw or not to draw. But if you draw, you will draw the right card—the more certainly, the more wilfully obstinate your behaviour." [78; italics mine]

IL EST INTERDIT D'INTERDIRE

As the reader will notice, the italicized parts of Cipolla's inductions are replete with repetitious word games, confusing double meanings, subtle injunctions, and self-reflexive paradoxes. Especially the latter are among the most powerful change-producing communications known to us. Their origins, too, reach far back into the past, but their first systematic formulation can be found in the article "Toward a Theory of Schizophrenia" [10], published by Bateson and his collaborators in 1956, and introducing the concept of the *double bind.* Since then the literature on this subject has proliferated,* and in order to avoid tiring repetitions, a short recapitulation may suffice to introduce some related but less well known concepts and interventions.

Paradox is the Achilles heel of our logical, analytical, rational world view. It is the point at which the seemingly all-embracing division of reality into pairs of opposites, especially into the Aristotelian dichotomy of true and false, breaks down and reveals itself as inadequate.† The French expression, *Il est interdit d'interdire,* is a good example of a paradoxical injunction: The prohibition to prohibit, prohibit *anything,* is, of course, itself a prohibition and creates a logically and practically untenable situation, because by prohibiting it self-reflexively contradicts itself. For if all prohibitions are prohibited, then also the prohibition to prohibit itself is prohibited; which means that one may prohibit. But if one may, then it is prohibited, for the prohibition to pro-

---

* Cf [116, pp. 187–229]; [117, pp. 62–73]; [115, pp. 17–26]; and especially [105].

† For the reader interested in problems of logic, it should be mentioned that important steps toward the resolution of this dilemma have been made in the mathematical theory of groups and in cybernetics. Of particular importance in this connection I consider Brown's *Laws of Form* [17] and Varela's "Calculus for Self-Reference" [111].

hibit obviously includes *all* prohibitions, therefore also itself . . . and so on *ad infinitum*.

It is unlikely that this theoretical example will ever create practical havoc. But of concrete importance is that whole class of injunctions whose common denominator is the often-quoted "Be spontaneous!" paradox. It commonly arises in an interpersonal context in which one partner demands or expects of the other a behavior which can only arise spontaneously but not on command: The demand makes impossible that which is demanded. The most important clinical manifestation of the "Be spontaneous!" paradox is probably the prohibition of sadness and the implied message: "Be happy!" But it is just as impossible to enforce happiness as it is to forget sadness on command. The effect on the recipient of this message is a painful feeling of hopelessness, of being unable to do anything right in order to be approved of, in short: of depression. However, this outcome is only possible if he does not question the validity of the message itself but submits to it—otherwise it would have no power over him. But this means that—as clinical experience shows—he eventually imposes this paradox on himself and thus internalizes the demand for spontaneity which originally came from the outside. The more he now tries to awaken within himself the "right" feelings of joy and happiness, the more powerfully the paradox will influence him and the deeper he is likely to sink into his depression. Not essentially different from his predicament is the experience of the insomniac who also tries to reach the spontaneous phenomenon *sleep* by an act of willpower. He, too, places himself in a "Be spontaneous!" paradox which makes impossible just that which he wants to achieve.

Blocking the Left Hemisphere

SYMPTOM PRESCRIPTIONS

With this brief recapitulation we can now take a look at another therapeutic intervention. Whoever suffers from the inability to do something that he would like to do or, vice versa, from the compulsion to do something that he would like to avoid—in short: whoever has a symptom—finds himself in an analogous situation. We experience symptoms as inhibitions or as impulses outside our control, and in this sense totally spontaneous. This, however, suggests that the principle of *similia similibus curantur* may be applicable here. For if the deliberate attempt to be happy causes depression, and the effort to fall asleep keeps us awake, it stands to reason that the voluntary, deliberate performance of seemingly uncontrollable behaviors should deprive them of their spontaneity. This indeed seems to be the case and the appropriate therapeutic intervention thus consists in the prescription of—and not the traditional struggle against—the symptom.

Medicine men, shamans, and other unusual experts on the workings of the human mind, from the dawn of mankind to Carlos Castañeda's teacher, Don Juan, have probably always used this intervention. Viktor Frankl has called it the paradoxical intention and has described it repeatedly in his works (for example, [37]). The oldest reference known to me from the literature is the description of a case of impotence in *A Treatise on the Veneral Disease* by the famous English physician John Hunter (1728–1793):

A gentleman told me, that he had lost his powers. . . . After above an hour's investigation of the case, I made out the following facts; that he had at unnecessary times strong erections, which showed that he had naturally this power; that the erections were accompanied with desire, which are all the natural powers wanted; but that there was still a defect somewhere, which I supposed to be from the mind. I inquired if all women were alike to him, his answer was no; some women he could have connection with, as well as ever. This brought the defect, whatever it was, into a smaller compass; and it appeared that there was but one woman that produced this inability and that it arose from a desire to perform the act with this woman well; which desire produced in the mind doubt, or fear of the want of success, which was the cause of the inability of performing the act. As this arose entirely from the state of the mind, produced by a particular circumstance, the mind was to be applied to for the cure; and I told him that he might be cured, if he could perfectly rely on his own power of self-denial. When I explained what I meant, he told me that he could depend upon every act of his will, or resolution; I then told him, if he had a perfect confidence in himself in that respect, that he was to go to bed with this woman, but first to promise to himself, that he would not have any connection with her, for six nights, let his inclinations and powers be what they would; which he engaged to do; and also to let me know the result. About a fortnight after he told me that this resolution had produced such a total alteration in the state of his mind, that the power soon took place, for instead of going to bed with the fear of inability, he went with fears that he should be possessed with too much desire, too much power, so as to become uneasy to him, which really happened; for he would have been happy to have shortened the time; and when he had once broke the spell, the mind and powers went on together; his mind never returning to its former state. [59]

What this example teaches us has validity for virtually all symptom prescriptions. The conscious effort to produce a reaction that can only occur spontaneously either makes impossible its occurrence or produces abnormal, unplanned, and unwanted reactions instead. In either case, the problem is due to the attempted solution—that is, to some voluntary but abortive effort. This pseudosolution, *not* the unwanted reaction that occurs or the desired action that fails to take place, must therefore become the target of therapeutic intervention. Very probably the problem-engendering "solution" (without which the "problem" would not even exist), this self-defeating application of conscious will power falls into the domain of the left hemisphere. The symptom prescription interdicts the attempted solution and with it its consequence, the symptom.*

Again some practical examples:

In a marriage therapy the husband complains that his very insecure wife has been asking him over and over again: "Do you still love me?", and is driving him to distraction with statements like: "I know that you will leave me." The wife admits doing this but is unable to supply a reason for her behavior, except her general nervousness and pessimism. She is quite aware of the fact that her repeated doubts about his affection are leaving him impatient, angry, and indeed unloving, and that her expectation to be abandoned by him may eventually turn into a self-fulfilling prophecy. In accordance with this the husband reports that he has so far attempted the only solution that to him appears reasonable—that is, to assuage her anxious insecurity and to help her through kind, supportive encouragement. He goes on to say that this usually, but not always, reassures her for a short time, but that she soon starts to drill these questions into him again. Faced with this situation, the therapist can take one of two very different approaches: He can either himself start drilling for the deepseated, intrapsychic reasons for this woman's behavior, or he can deal with the problem from the point of view of this couple's interaction. In this latter case he will readily see that they are caught in a "Be spontaneous!" paradox and that the obvious target for an intervention is the husband's attempted solution—

---

* As long as we maintain the traditional, "horizontal" separation between conscious and unconscious, this explanation seems to turn the concept of pathogenesis upside down: The conscious rather than the unconscious mind appears to be the origin of the symptom. If, on the other hand, we can accept the idea of a "vertical" separation between the two halves of the brain (the modern equivalent of Janet's dissociation theory, referred to briefly in the foregoing) there is no theoretical discrepancy.

that is, his earnest and sincere efforts to convince her once and for all. In an individual interview he is instructed to stop these attempts and to agree with her smilingly "Of course, I do not love you and shall certainly leave you soon." The rest is laughter.

Very much like this husband, a therapist may also commit the mistake of trying to bring an inhibited, reticent patient to greater trust and self-disclosure. Far more effective than these efforts is the Ericksonian technique of insisting: "Please, don't tell me anything that you do not want me to know until you are really ready to talk about it." Or: "I do not want you to talk about this today—maybe not even by the end of next week."

In this connection also the *"worst fantasy" technique* should be mentioned. It enables the therapist to approach a very tabooed or otherwise anxiety-producing subject without the client's full awareness by asking him not to talk about his "real" fear, but to try to imagine the most disastrous, most unlikely consequences that his problem could possibly lead to. Thus exonerated from the bounds of the real, possible, and reasonable, most people find it easier to envisage, and talk about, the real, possible outcomes. As can be seen, this intervention, too, is the exact opposite of what "common sense" would dictate.

Bandler and Grinder mention a patient, the participant in a group therapy session, whose symptom was that she could not say "no." Not surprisingly, this inability was the cause of stereotypical problems, from material exploitation all the way into the sexual area. But in her world image the act of denying was associated with far worse consequences than these. She claimed that as a child she had once refused to stay home with her father and upon her return had found him dead. Since then she was terrified of the magical consequences of any denial and avoided it.*

---

* Avoidance as the "best possible" solution of a problem creates a very interesting vicious circle. The nonoccurrence of the feared event, as the supposed result of its avoid-

Blocking the Left Hemisphere

In front of the group the therapist imposed a double bind by asking her to say "no" about something to every member of the group. She reacted strongly and refused to carry out the task. "No! It's impossible for me to say 'no' to people! You can't expect me to do it just because you ask me to" [7, pp. 170–71]. After several minutes of this agitated refusal and only after the therapist pointed out to her that she had been saying "no" to him all this time did she realize that she had indeed been denying something without any dire consequences.

The structure of this elegant symptom prescription (which is the basis of every successful therapeutic double bind) is thus:

1. Symptom: "I cannot say 'no'."
2. Symptom prescription: "Say 'no' to everyone present!"
3. Double bind: Two alternatives (either to say "no" to everybody or to say "no" to the therapist) which both lead to the desired outcome.

Thus, while in a pathogenic double bind one is—as the saying goes—"damned if he does and damned if he doesn't" (cf. the example given on page 108), in a therapeutic double bind the client is "changed if he does and changed if he doesn't" carry out the prescription.

The structure will occupy us again in the section on the illusion of alternatives.

---

ance, reinforces the belief into the necessity and the effectiveness of the avoidance. But by doing this the avoider deprives himself of the possibility of ever discovering that the feared event would not occur even without the ritual of avoidance. Thus the supposed solution becomes the problem, and therapy must be applied to this "solution" and not to the alleged "problem" (for example, the results of a childhood experience). (The subject is dealt with in greater detail in [117, pp. 31–39].)

Cf. also the old joke of the man who claps his hands every ten seconds. Asked for the reason for this strange behavior, he says: "To chase away the elephants." "Elephants? But there aren't any around." "You see!?"

SYMPTOM DISPLACEMENTS

About halfway between these symptom prescriptions and the re-framing of problems (pages 118–26), there stands the technique of deliberately induced symptom displacements. This intervention does not attempt to influence a symptom directly, but rather aims at its provisional shift which, however, if successful makes the patient aware of the fact that his seemingly uncontrollable symptom can be influenced after all.

This technique, too, has been applied in hypnotherapy for a long time and is used there above all for the alleviation of pain whose intensity is known to be greatly dependent on subjective, contextual, and especially interpersonal factors. There are two ways in which this can be accomplished: shifts in *time* (for example, "Your pain will concentrate itself on Monday, Wednesday, and Friday evenings from eight to nine") or in *space* (for example, "Your pain will slowly descend from your hip through the left knee into your left foot"). More about this technique can be found in any textbook of clinical hypnosis.

But there exists a third possibility. It is the deliberate use of a symptom instead of its passive endurance. This amounts to a shift of its significance and this effect brings it—as mentioned above—close to the technique of reframing. As I want to deal with the latter separately, let me quote here only one typical case of symptom displacement:

Erickson once treated a sexually very inhibited woman who had been married for nine years but had never lost her original fear of intercourse. Her symptom consisted in rather severe attacks of choking and gasping during, but often also before, love-making. From his detailed description of this treatment, I want to quote only that part in which Erickson mentions how—in accordance with the rule of the unresolved remnant—he arrived at the agreement with the patient that she would save her symptom for other, more useful purposes. He explains his intervention as follows:

How many patients resent your taking their difficulty away from them? How many bottled chronic appendices are there in the family treasures? Have you ever listened to someone tell you, "This is the appendix the doctor took out. Do you know how many attacks I had of appendicitis?" They treasure their problem, but they want to treasure it safely. What I was saying to her was, "Let's put your choking and gasping into a speci-men bottle of some kind—and you can have it, it's yours." She told me what she wanted her choking and gasping behavior for. She said, "There is a couple that have been friends of ours for a long time, and I don't like them. They always come and they always want drinks and they always drink too much. They always find fault unless we have the best whiskey. Joe likes them. I don't like them. . . . I want to get rid of them. I don't want them to be friends of ours." Every time that couple came to call, she had a choking and gasping episode, and now she is rid of them. [53, pp. 257–58]

As a result of this paradoxical symptom prescription and its dis-placement from the original context (sex) to the situation with the other couple, the patient was free from her symptom as soon as she had managed to free herself (by means of the displaced symp-tom) of the other couple. In this type of intervention, too, we are struck by the fact that the phenomen—symptom displace-ment—has been known for a long time, but only as a negative, undesirable complication and not also as a deliberately applied therapeutic process.

THE ILLUSION OF ALTERNATIVES

In a well-known story the judge asks the defendant: "Have you stopped beating your wife?" and threatens him with a contempt of court charge because the latter will not answer "yes" or "no," but tries to explain that the judge's question does not apply, since he has *never* beaten his wife. From the point of view of formal logic this not at all improbable story is very interesting. The judge's question would be appropriate if it could be shown that the accused is indeed beating his wife or, at least, that he has done so in the past. If this were the case, then there would only be the two possibilities envisaged by the judge: Either the man has stopped beating his wife or he is still beating her. In this frame there is no third possibility—and this brings us back to the *tertium non datur* of Aristotelian logic. As is known, this is a logic of alternatives (from Latin *alter*: the second, or other, of two), of which one obtains (is "true," or "real," and so forth) and the other therefore does not hold. For within this frame nothing can either be both (true *and* false) or neither (neither true *nor* false). Admittedly, Aristotelian logic is somewhat more sophisticated than that but, by and large, this is the logic by which we order our everyday life. The trouble is that on the one hand it is only too easy to violate this logic but that, on the other hand, the results of these violations may play havoc, especially in our interpersonal relations, and trigger off rather irrational reactions. Conceivably, the above-mentioned accused may tear out his hair, insult the judge, or go home and actually beat up his wife— but to grasp intellectually what has happened may not be easy at all for him.

This pattern of communication was first identified by Weakland and Jackson in schizophrenic family interaction and called

the *illusion of alternatives* [118]. As the name and the above example suggest, this pattern is based on a forced choice between
two alternatives, a choice which is illusory because neither the
one nor the other alternative obtains, is permitted or is, for one
reason or another, practically possible. The person trapped in this
illusion is, therefore, again "damned if he does and damned if he
doesn't."

Some examples:

1.   "Heads I win, tails you lose" goes a well-known expression
which creates the illusion that a choice will be left to the impar-
tial decision of fate by throwing a coin. Only upon closer examination does it become evident that the two alternatives are illusory, for on the basis of this formula (whose chiastic structure
makes it sound even more convincing) the partner will lose in *either* case. In other words, for him this frame does not contain the
possibility of winning.

2.   From a family psychotherapy session, Laing reports the
following dialogue between a mother and her schizophrenic
daughter:

Mother:	I don't blame you for talking that way. I know you don't re-ally mean it.
Daughter:	But I do mean it.
Mother:	Now dear, I know you don't, you can't help yourself.
Daughter:	I can help myself.
Mother:	Now dear, I know you can't because you're ill. If I thought for a moment you weren't ill I would be furious with you. [74]

The way the mother sees her daughter's behavior, there are
only two alternatives: madness or badness.

3.   In disturbed family interaction we frequently observe
that—quite reasonably—the parents expect of their child that he

become independent of them and begin to live a life of his own, *but* that, on the other hand, they interpret any step that their child may make in that direction as a sign of ingratitude, disaffection, or even treason. Thus, no matter whether he remains dependent or attempts to become independent, he is wrong and a bad son.

4. Alcoholic men are very anxious to be seen by their families as loving, respectable husbands and fathers. If such a man returns home drunk, his relatives can only react in one of two ways: Remembering past incidents of violence on similar occasions, they may either betray their (only too justified) fear of renewed brutality, in which case he is likely to react violently for their fear implies that they do not see him as their loving, considerate spouse and parent; or they may try to hide their fear, in which case he may attack them for their "insincerity."*

5. A common aspect of the paranoid's world view consists in seeing further evidence for the sinister intentions of others in their efforts to assure him that they are not out to hurt him and only have his best interests at heart. It therefore does not matter how the others try to react to his suspicions, for whatever they do, they feed into them.

6. Searles describes several typical patterns of communication which he aptly calls "efforts to drive the other person crazy." According to him one can achieve this, for instance, by treating one and the same subject in a humorous and then, the next time, in a dead-serious fashion, blaming the partner for ei-

* Even though the following is not directly related to our subject, it may be worth mentioning that there exists, after all, one escape from this untenable situation: One could imagine that one of his children might run away, claiming that there is a huge, black gorilla breathing fire in the house. This metaphor, which says something to the effect: "You are a terrifying monster, smelling of liquor," would in turn place the father in an untenable situation, for on the one hand the child "obviously" is not talking about him and, on the other hand, what father who loves his child would blame him for a mere imagination? In orthodox psychopathology, such a counter-paradox is called a hallucination.

ther having no sense of humor or for being flippant about a serious matter. Similarly, by behaving seductively in a social situation that excludes any erotic behavior one can accuse the other—depending on his/her reaction—of being either sexually inhibited or impudent; *tertium non datur* [100].

All these examples show that in an illusion of alternatives there appear to exist two choices, but that in actual fact they are not true alternatives and that, in spite of their seeming difference, they constitute only *one* pole of a superordinate pair of opposites. This meta-opposition is not easy to describe. Let us return to the example of the judge and the accused: The latter means the meta-opposition, namely that which exists between beating and not-beating. The judge, acting from the power position of his authority, negates *a priori* the possibility of not-beating (and, therefore, of *never*-having-beaten), and thus leaves only the two alternatives *no-longer*-beating and *still*-beating. The way he draws the frame, both alternatives are fully contained in what, for the accused, is only *one half* of the pair of opposites that he means (namely, beating and not-beating, respectively).

Or to return once more to the slogan "National Socialism or Bolshevik chaos?" It implies that the two concepts are absolute opposites and once this implication is made, the moral obligation to embrace the good, pure alternative and to reject the chaotic-diabolic alternative seems to follow quite logically. *Tertium non datur*—not because there really is no third possibility, but simply because it is not contained in the ideological framework of the slogan. In democratic view, both alternatives are as little different as, indeed, spuds and potatoes; both are totalitarian and the purported difference is an illusion of alternatives. The figure on page 112 tries to illustrate this: The bar-bell-shaped configuration in the left circle is meant to represent the pair of opposites composed of National Socialism and Bolshevism. They are entirely con-

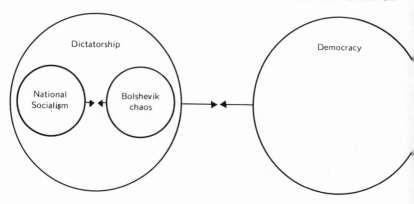

tained within the area of *dictatorship* (the left circle) which is the opposite of *democracy* (the right circle). The two larger circles together thus form a meta-pair of opposites.* This means, however, that the illusion of alternatives vanishes the moment we become aware of the superordinate opposition. Consequently, this realization must be suppressed and is therefore subject to punishment. The Gestapo's reaction was thus not only directed at the irreverent way in which this pearl of totalitarian *raison d'état* had been derided but additionally at the "think crime" of becoming aware of the *existence of the meta-alternative* and of breaking out of the frame. This escape is prevented by metaphorical or literal walls and barbed wire fences, and in this connection it appears ironic that the concept of *mystification* should originally have been coined by Marx. In the example of the imaginary judge the defendant is threatened with contempt of court; in a dictatorship a political joke is considered subversive; and in the

* Regardless of whether or not one is acquainted with Hegelian dialectics, the intriguing question now arises: If this representation is correct, what prevents us from placing the meta-pair of opposites (in our case dictatorship and democracy, respectively) into a yet more comprehensive frame (circle) and to consider this frame the *one* half of a metameta-pair of opposites and not, in Hegel's sense, as the synthesis that transcends the opposition of thesis and antithesis? But what then is *its* alternative and what is this opposition all about? At this point our inquiry obviously becomes metaphysical.

Blocking the Left Hemisphere

families of schizophrenics any move of the identified patient to-wards normalcy is seen as further evidence of his craziness.*

But again we discover that this form of communication has not only pathogenic but also therapeutic potential. The latter shall now be presented in some detail.

Erickson [30] reports that as a young boy he had to work on his father's farm and that he was often placed by his father into what I would call an illusion of alternatives by being permitted to decide "freely" whether, for instance, he wanted to feed the chickens first or the hogs. The illusion was evidently concealed behind the innocent word "first," for he was not free to choose whether he wanted to feed the animals *at all*—this possibility simply did not exist and was, therefore, not even mentioned—but only which of the two chores (which *both* had to be done) he wanted to tackle *first*. (The figure on page 114 illustrates the structure of this illusion. The reader will readily see that it is identical with that shown on page 112.)

Erickson also remembers that he later began to use this method himself in college, inducing his fellow students into a choice between two tasks, *both* of which they would have rejected without hesitation if they had been presented to them *singly*. In Erickson's own words, they would "execute one or the other if I

---

* Cf. Laing and Esterson's report on a patient whose interaction with her family they observed through the psychotic episode:

So far June has held her own. Her mother continues to express herself in extremely ambivalent terms over evidences of June's greater independence. She tells her she looks hideous when wearing ordinary make-up, she actively ridicules her expectancy that any boy is interested in her, she treats any expressions of irritation or exasperation on June's part as symptoms of the "illness," or construes them as tokens of "evil". . . .

She [June] has to keep a tight control on herself, however, because if she shouts, screams, cries, swears, eats too little, or eats too much, eats too fast, or eats too slowly, reads too much, sleeps too much or too little, her mother tells her that she is ill. It takes a lot of courage on June's part to take the risk of not being what her parents call "well." [75]

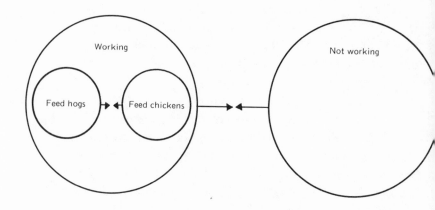

made the refusal of one contingent upon the acceptance of the other." But he also noticed that the ultimate reactions were unfavorable if he used these double binds for his personal advantage, while he achieved lasting, positive effects when he employed them for the other person's benefit.*

The illusion of alternatives is an important part of many trance inductions. For instance:

"Would you like to go into a trance now or later?"

"Do you want to have your eyes open or closed when you experience trance?"

---

* Although the following remarks are not immediately related to the above, it might be useful to mention here briefly the expedience of offering *true* alternatives in marital therapy. In the world image of most men it is an expression of love, kindness, and fairness to offer their wives free and unconditional choice regarding some joint undertaking. They are therefore deeply hurt when their wives not only do not react with gratitude but with annoyance, retorting for instance: "If *everything* I want is all right, then *nothing* I want really matters to you." For him this is crying illogic and a distortion of his best intentions, and may lead to conflicts even in the most trivial situations. A change can frequently be brought about by getting the husband to offer her at least two possibilities to choose from: for example, two restaurants, two plays, two vacation resorts. She now feels that he is genuinely trying to find out what she really wants to have or to do; at the same time she is offered a concrete choice; and, finally, nothing prevents her from making a counter-suggestion if neither of the alternatives proposed by him are to her liking.

Blocking the Left Hemisphere

"Will your right hand lift or press down or move to the side first? Or will it be your left? Let's just wait and see which it will be."

"Will your eyelids grow heavy and close or will they remain comfortable and open in that one position?"

Or an even more intricate double bind: "If your unconscious wants you to enter trance your right hand will lift. Otherwise your left will lift." [30, p. 152]

The obvious common denominator of all these examples is that the occurrence of trance is implied in them as an unquestionable certainty; what remains to be seen is merely when, under what circumstances, with what additional manifestations it will occur—but not *if* it will occur. This is especially true of the last example, whose peculiar logic even appears to leave open the question whether the subject will go into a trance *or not*—except that the evidence for the occurrence of this second alternative is itself a trance phenomenon and thus completes the paradox.

The skillful use of illusions of alternatives may help parents to get over many of those typical difficulties and power struggles with their children:

"Do you wish to take a bath before going to bed or would you rather put your pajamas on in the bathroom?"

"Do you want to go to bed at a quarter to eight or at eight o'clock?" [30, p. 145]

All this does not mean to purport that an illusion of alternatives will only succeed in trance or with children, but not with adults whose critical reason, at least in their waking state, would make them immune against this intervention. This view would turn the causality of the phenomenon upside down. It is not an (already existing) impairment of our critical faculties which makes possible the illusion, but rather the illusion blocks the critical-analytic functions of the left hemisphere. For this reason the technique of creating illusionary alternatives has its place and its importance also in general psychotherapy. For instance, if it appears desirable to stress at a certain point the expectability of imminent change, one can either do this in the intellectual language of the left hemisphere or—much more effectively—by means of the seemingly absurd question: "Do you want to gain control over your problem already this week or the next? That is probably too soon. Perhaps you prefer a longer pause—maybe three or four weeks?" Notice here the ambiguity of the word *pause:* Is that supposed to mean that it is in the patient's power to postpone the intimated improvement (which implies that he has indeed control over his symptom and could, therefore, just as well improve it today), or that there will occur a pause of the *problem* (which again insinuates that it can be resolved)?

What all these interventions have in common is that, almost by a sleight of hand, a specific frame is created which excludes the undesirable outcome. Within this frame an illusionary choice is then offered between two possibilities, *both* of which are aspects of the desired goal of treatment. If it is not possible to establish this illusionary frame, the intervention will have no effect. If I ask a stranger: "Would you rather give me one or ten dollars?" my question will fall flat because he will have no difficulty rejecting both alternatives. But if I ask the same question within the frame of, say, a fund-raising event, my chances of getting at least one dollar are fairly good.

It goes without saying—and is, incidentally, a frequently stated doubt about the effectiveness of this intervention—that the success of every therapeutic illusion of alternatives is in jeopardy if the subject either does not enter at all into the frame drawn by the therapist, or decides to leave it. Especially in hypnotherapy, the latter is quite often the case. The experienced hypnotist meets this difficulty by a skilled and immediate enlargement of the original frame to the point where it includes the resistance or other nontrance behavior in question. If, for instance, he has tried unsuccessfully to bring about a hand levitation and the hand remains motionless and heavy,* he can then reframe it as evidence that the subject is already in a much deeper trance than he thought. At least in theory one can thus redefine any failure as proof of success; in practice the limits are determined here, too, by the therapist's inventiveness and presence of mind. Or, to put it another way: A situation is created deliberately against which Karl Popper [90] advisedly warns in science and especially in research; that is, a conceptual frame is used which cannot be refuted. In Popper's sense this is a system that cannot be falsified and in which both success *and* failure "prove" the correctness of the basic premise.

But let us return once more to the pathological illusions of alternatives. We saw that here the world image in question does not contain the meta-alternative. There are only two possibilities and both are unacceptable, impossible, or prohibited. Where this problem exists, its solution—and therefore also the task of therapy—lies in gaining access to a superordinate alternative,† and this always consists in transcending the seemingly inescapable pseudoalternatives imposed from outside. And this leads to my next subject.

---

* For simplicity's sake, we shall disregard here the fact that hypnotic suggestions of motor activity often fail, but that this does not exclude that the subject is already in trance.

† The most beautiful illustration of this form of solution, known to me, is the story of the Wife of Bath in Chaucer's *Canterbury Tales*. It describes how in trying to make the "right" choice a knight gets more and more deeply enmeshed in difficulties by falling a victim to ever new illusions of alternatives, until he finally refuses to choose one of the two alternatives offered but rejects *the need to choose itself.* The same thought is expressed by Karl Kraus in one of his aphorisms: "If I have to choose the lesser of two evils, I shall choose neither." But above all we are reminded of Pascal's famous remark: Both he who chooses heads and he who chooses tails are equally at fault. They are both in the wrong. The true course is not to wager at all.

REFRAMING

When Alexander the Great simply cut through the knot by which Gordius, the king of Phrygia, had tied the yoke to the shaft of his chariot, he proved that the solution of a problem depends on how one sees it. For Alexander the task was to separate the yoke from the shaft, but not to *untie* the knot which many people before him had tried and failed to do. The difference between the two definitions of the problem may appear trivial, but is actually decisive for its solution.

If an armed robber demands somebody's wallet, the victim appears to have only two alternatives: to give in or to resist. Both are highly unpleasant, but the first is the lesser evil, and the robber knows and exploits this. But let us imagine that the victim has nerves of steel and manages to give a totally new meaning to the situation by telling the thug: "I have been looking for somebody like you for a long time. You can now either take my wallet—it contains twenty dollars. Or, you can earn twenty-thousand by putting my wife's lover out of commission. If you are interested, come see me tomorrow and we can work out the details." Through this simple, albeit not absolutely foolproof method the victim has extricated himself from an apparently untenable position and gained the upper hand by offering two completely different alternatives. And yet, the scenario as such has remained unchanged: A victim who seems to have money; a *desperado* who has none and who seems to have no qualms about a human life. But instead of the alternative: "Your wallet or your life (and your wallet)," the choice is now: "Twenty or twenty-thousand dollars."

And finally, once again the humorous but by no means trivial definition of the difference between an optimist and a pessimist:

Blocking the Left Hemisphere

The optimist says of a bottle that it is half full; the pessimist sees it as half empty. The same bottle and the same quantity of wine, in other words: The same first-order reality—but two very different world images, creating two very different (second-order) "realities."

In this changeability of subjective "realities" lies the power of those therapeutic interventions that have come to be known under the rubric of reframing. Let us remember: We never deal with reality *per se*, but rather with *images* of reality—that is, with interpretations. While the number of potentially possible interpretations is very large, our world image usually permits us to see only one—and this *one* therefore appears to be the only possible, reasonable, and permitted view. Furthermore, this one interpretation also suggests only one possible, reasonable, and permitted solution, and if we don't succeed at first we try and try again—or, in other words, we resort to the recipe of doing *more of the same* [117, pp. 31–39]. This is where reframing comes in and is successful if it manages to invest a given situation with a new meaning that is just as appropriate or even more convincing than the one our client has so far attributed to it. That this meaning must be congenial to his world image and communicated to him in the "language" of this image shall, although obvious, be explained in some detail in Chapter 8.

To avoid misunderstandings, however, it should be emphasized at this point that a reframing is not an interpretation in the classic psychotherapeutic sense; it "deciphers" nothing and does not uncover the "true" meaning hidden behind allegoric, symbolic, or bizarre facades. Since I have presented the logical basis of reframing in greater detail elsewhere [117, pp. 92–109], I want to avoid tedious repetitions and deal here mainly with the relation between the technique of reframing and the therapeutic illusion of alternatives. We saw that the latter consists in establishing a frame within which a seemingly free choice is offered between two alternatives, both of which amount to the same outcome—that is, therapeutic change. An illusion is thus created, suggesting that there are only these two possibilities, or—in other words—a state of blindness is produced for the fact that there indeed exist other possibilities *outside* the frame. *Reframing goes in the opposite direction.* It breaks the illusionary frame inherent in any world image, and thereby reveals that what appeared unchangeable can indeed be changed and that there exist superordinate alternatives. Some practical examples shall illustrate this:

In *The Doctor and the Soul* [36], and in his talks, Viktor Frankl refers to the possibility of reframing a frequently encountered problem—namely, the deep, all-pervading grief produced by the death of a beloved person. Life has lost its meaning; everything that was beautiful and worth living for has left this world together with the deceased—and within this frame only the return of the dead could again lend sense to one's own life. (Of course, the very fact that this person is seeking help contradicts his seemingly all-embracing hopelessness on a higher level.) Frankl reframes the situation by asking the patient to imagine that, while Frankl cannot of course bring the deceased back to life, he would introduce him to another person who not only physically but also otherwise resembles the dead person in every respect; who is so completely informed about the life of the deceased that together they would be able to recall and discuss every detail of their joint experiences—would the patient accept this person as a valid substitute? In attempting to answer this question the patient is forced to look at his loss from a perspective that lies outside the vicious, closed circle of his grief. Frankl reports that his patient usually rejects the illusionary alternative, and it seems to me that in achieving this rejection Frankl has produced a decisive change in the patient's world image: He has gently brought the sufferer closer to accepting the irreversibility of the beloved person's death and thereby has created some distance to it.

A thumb-sucker usually limits his efforts to one thumb and changes to the other only if sucking the first is somehow made impossible or unpleasant. But sucking he does, no matter how much his parents may try to stop him. A useful intervention, combining elements of symptom prescription and of reframing, consists in pointing out to him, in clear, understandable language and in his mother's presence, that we live in a democratic society in which everybody has the same rights and that it is therefore not right to suck only one finger at the exclusion of the other nine. He is enjoined to suck every one of the other fingers just as long as his thumb, and the mother is advised to make sure, if necessary with the help of a clock, that all fingers are democratically granted their equal privileges. What until then was a pleasurable activity that had the additional advantage of needling the helpless parents now is transformed into a duty whose fulfillment quickly becomes an annoying chore—especially since it takes place under parental supervision. But this reframing also offers a face-saving way out of the dilemma: It permits the child to suck less or not at all. What is more, it blocks the parents' usual problem-perpetuating solutions, such as shaming, threatening, punishing, and the like.

It is a typical problem of many students that they cannot concentrate their attention on study matters because they are distracted by almost incessant thoughts about the many, much more pleasant things they could do if they did not have to study. They then try unsuccessfully to force themselves to concentrate, and this self-imposed torture often lasts late into their nights and begins again early in the morning. Frequently an almost immediate improvement can be achieved if they can be brought to set themselves a reasonable time limit for the completion of their daily tasks, after which limit they may do anything they want to do *except* studying. Leisure and pleasure are thus reframed as a punishment and thereby lose their charm in very much the same way as we may find ourselves wide awake on Sunday mornings, while on work days we could sleep for hours and hours.

An intelligent student finds it increasingly difficult to keep up with his study requirements. It turns out that he has placed himself under a double "Be spontaneous!" paradox. First of all, he is convinced that because of his interest in his chosen subjects he ought to *like* studying them and, since he does not, there must be something the matter with him. Secondly, he knows that his studying places considerable financial burdens on his parents. This makes him feel very guilty about his poor academic achievements but also about the fact that he does not experience *sincere* gratitude for their help and even somehow resents having to be grateful. Faced with this situation, a therapist can now either try to uncover whatever hidden reasons and causes may lie behind the complications just described, or he can reframe the student's attitude as unrealistic and immature: Even under the best of circumstances studying is an unpleasant necessity and to believe that it should be gratifying is simply ridiculous. As far as his parents are concerned, they have a right to his gratitude but this does not mean that he has to *like* having to be thankful. He can then leave it up to the student to continue in his immature outlooks or to have the adult courage to reject them and to begin to look at life as a mixture of pleasant and unpleasant things.

Another student who has never been away from home before is running into the usual difficulties: He has not yet made new friends, he finds it difficult to manage his money, dislikes the many new rules and regulations, and misses the comforts of life at home. At the same time, however, he sees nothing unusual in all of this and is quite willing to try to get used to it. The real problem appears to be his mother, who has always overprotected him and who has not yet resigned herself to not having him around any more. In her daily telephone calls she keeps suggesting that he should feel free to come back home if the situation becomes too unpleasant. This not only complicates and prolongs his period of adjustment but actually increases the chances of his giving up and dropping out of school. She consults a therapist who has little difficulty realizing that all she wants is for him to agree with her that she is handling the situation correctly, and that he would not see her again if he were to try to point out to her what her husband, her own parents, her older sons, and several friends have already insisted on: namely, that her overprotection has negative effects on the boy. In the latter's presence the therapist therefore reframes the situation by painstakingly pointing out that one of the most important tasks of motherhood consists in preparing her children for the difficulties of adult life—an argument which she of course fully supports. He then goes on to lecture that the success of this task is measured by the ability of the son to leave his parents' home, and that this separation is psychologically of such overriding importance for his future and his self-confidence as a male that it must not be made too easy for him. This would deprive him of the comfortable, reassuring realization that he can function even under adverse circumstances. Behind all this the mother smells the well-known rat of the stereotypical admonition to let the boy sink or swim and not to entice him into coming home again. What she, therefore, least expects is the therapist's instruction to make it maximally difficult for her son to achieve his separation from home by making it as enticing as possible for him to drop out of school—only by managing to resist these temptations will he be able to approach future difficulties with some degree of confidence into his abilities to cope. Whether they accept and like it or not, the situation is now completely reframed for both of them and the mother is in a double bind: To pamper and overprotect the son has now been defined as an important maternal duty; at the same time, it is implied that she might thereby bring him close to failure, but this, too, would be desirable, because it would teach him a useful lesson regarding the importance of self-reliance. The mother now has only two alternatives to choose from. She can either continue to try and make things easy for her son, which, however, "really" means that she is making his life difficult, or she must stop pampering him. This second alternative seems all the more compelling to her if she considers the therapist's instruction to be a specially harsh, even cruel method of education of which, on the other hand, it cannot be denied that its goal is her son's well-being and his ability to cope with life problems. This reframing creates the preconditions for change of which Wittgenstein once said that we cannot continue to play a game after somebody has taught us a new game instead of the old one. "But how can the new game have made the old one obsolete?—We now see something different and can no longer naively go on playing" [121].

This example also shows that reframing must not necessarily be positive or even acceptable. In fact, it can be particularly effective to reframe a situation, a behavior, or other set of circumstances in a way which to the client seems unacceptable, wrong, or outright stupid. This is especially the case when it is not only so incompatible with his world image that it actually challenges him into proving its falseness, but when this proof makes it necessary to engage in the very behavior which is the goal of therapy. More will be said about this in the section on resistance; at this point a practical example may help to clarify the nature of this intervention:

Blocking the Left Hemisphere

My colleague Dr. Fisch, who is consultant to a local juvenile hall, was recently confronted with the following problem. A 12-year-old inmate habitually disrupted classes by constant talking and other undisciplined behavior. When he did this, he was usually sent to his room. Of late he had refused to stay there and it had become necessary to lock him in it. To this he had begun to respond with an escalation, banging against the door with his fists and his feet—if necessary for hours on end. The staff in turn then resorted to a further escalation by taking him to the isolation cell in the basement. With this they had exhausted their possibilities, while the boy managed to continue his banging that could still be heard throughout the entire building. The situation became critical inasmuch as the boy had been sent to juvenile hall precisely on account of his uncontrollable behavior and it now became evident to all the other inmates that the staff were just as powerless to deal with it as were his parents and the school. It was therefore decided that the boy was a "psychiatric" case and my colleague was asked to treat him. He, however, saw in it a problem of interaction between the inmates and the authorities and completely reframed the situation by suggesting to the other children a game: Everybody was to guess exactly how long Joe would continue his banging, and the closest guess would be rewarded with a bottle of Coca-Cola. What my colleague had hoped would happen in one way or another did in fact occur: One of the other boys sneaked out of the class room, ran to the window of the isolation cell and shouted: "Joe, keep it up for another seven minutes and I win a bottle of Coke!" The banging stopped immediately.

It is also possible to communicate a reframing quite indirectly and in an apparently fortuitous and unintended way. Erickson was once consulted by a woman whose 14-year-old daughter had developed the conviction that her feet were grotesquely large and as a result of it had begun to withdraw from her friends, from school, and from most other activities outside the home. As can be imagined, everybody tried to convince her that her feet were perfectly normal and that the whole idea was just ridiculous. As a result of these well-meant, commonsensical exhortations, a typical game without end had established and consolidated itself between the girl and her human environment. The more the others tried to make her come to her senses, the more she insisted on the huge size of her feet. Erickson arranged for a home visit, the ostensible reason being a medical examination of the mother. In the course of this examination he had the girl fetch a towel and stand behind him, holding the towel ready in case he needed it. He then suddenly moved back, "inadvertently" stepping on one of her feet. As she cried out in pain he turned around and said angrily: "If you would grow these things *large* enough for a *man* to see, I wouldn't be in this sort of situation." Erickson reports that this one intervention was sufficient to bring about the desired change in the girl's body image.

Most of the examples contained in this chapter have a common denominator that so far has not been mentioned explicitly: They are based on direct prescriptions of certain behaviors. In these prescriptions there lies the third possibility of circumventing or blocking the logical, analytical censorship of the right hemisphere.

Injunctive Language—
Behavior Prescriptions

If you desire to see, learn how to act.
—Heinz von Foerster

IT OFTEN HAPPENS that the most immediately obvious is most difficult to grasp. What happens if we ask somebody to do something that he would not have considered doing at that time and on his own accord? To deal with this problem in its fundamental simplicity, let us for the moment leave aside the question as to *why* he should be willing to carry out such a command and *how* he can be motivated to do so. What needs to be investigated first is the mechanism of the command itself.

Surprisingly, very little is known about this, especially in the field of therapeutic communication. This is probably because in the monadic world image of traditional psychotherapy, with its taboo against referring to direct influence as direct influence and its fundamentally medical disease-model, there simply is no conceptual room for this sort of intervention. But if—as this book submits—the purpose of therapy is seen as a change of the patient's predominantly right-hemispheric world image, and if, supported by increasing experimental evidence, there is reason to assume that it is the reasonable, analytical faculties of the left hemisphere which will approve certain courses of action and reject others, then the perspective changes. It then begins to make sense to investigate the phenomena of everyday spontaneous changes and to identify the practical conclusions that may be drawn from them. This type of change—spontaneous change—obviously occurs when certain perceptions or other experiences can no longer be integrated into a person's world image (or even directly contradict it) and thus requires an at least partial change of the image. Provided that the discrepancy is not too frightening and therefore produces the opposite result—perceptual defense, denial, or even psychosis—one has made an experience, one has grown and matured.

Traditionally, this model of change is accepted as valid, but most therapists are trained to wait passively for the spontaneous occurrence of such events in the environment and/or the mind of their patients. But there is absolutely no reason why they may not be brought about actively—except that it violates a dogma of traditional psychotherapy. Here Einstein's famous remark to Heisenberg comes to mind: "It is the theory that determines what we can observe," which, applied to therapy and without doing it violence, may be paraphrased to read: "It is the theory which decides what we can do." In other words, what is possible and feasible in therapy is determined much more by the nature of the particular *doctrine* of therapy than by the nature of the human *mind*.

As already mentioned, commands as communicational phenomena in their own right have so far remained a rather ne-

glected area of linguistics and especially of semantics. But Condillac thought that speech may have had its origin in the
"language of action" and in recent years Jaynes, a psychologist at
Princeton University, postulated that commands are indeed
man's most archaic language forms. Combining brain-ana-
tomical evidence (obtained from endocasts of the skulls of the
Neanderthaler and other hominids) with meteorological data related to the last four glaciation periods, and with archeological
findings of tools and other implements used by early man, into
an elegant, far-reaching synthesis, he suggests the following: The
first manifestations of rudimentary speech were cries whose intensity was commensurate with the intensity of the danger. For
instance, a caveman might have indicated the approach of a tiger
by screaming "wahee!" while a more distant danger might have
been signalled by the shout "wahoo!" Gradually these different
endings may have become independent modifiers meaning *near*
and *far*. Jaynes suggests that the age of these modifiers lasted until
about the year 46,000 B.C. and that it was followed by the age of
commands, when "ee!" came to mean "come nearer!" and "oo!"
something like "go farther!" He believes that only on the basis of
these primordial digitalizations there gradually emerged and
evolved all the other elements of human speech (negations,
nouns, adjectives, and so on) [63].

The first modern logical theory of commands was proposed by
the Austrian philosopher Mally in 1926 under the title *Grundgesetze des Sollens* [Basic Laws of Commands] [77]. In the third part
of this book he deals specifically with the relation between voluntary action and its consequences and points out that willing—that
is, wishing to bring about—a certain outcome does not necessarily mean that one wills (wants) all the consequences following
from that act of will. In fact, some consequences are very likely to
emerge of which one may then say with full conviction: This I

did not want—or, I would add: This I did not expect. There is, then, an intimate relation between voluntary action and certain realizations that were inaccessible to the mind of the agent *before he took that action*; a cognitive component of action which von Foerster has succinctly expressed in his imperative: If you desire to see, learn how to act.

Basing himself on Mally's work, but going well beyond it, University of Pittsburgh philosopher Nicholas Rescher constructed his *Logic of Commands* [93]—that is, a logic of imperative sentences similar to the classic logic of the truth functions of indicative sentences. Rescher quotes the famous French mathematician Henri Poincaré, who categorically stated:

The principles of science, the postulates of geometry are, and can only be, in the indicative mood; and in this mood are also the experimental verities, and on the basis of science there is not, and there cannot be, anything else. . . . Therefore, even the most subtle dialectician may juggle these principles as he wishes, combine them, make them into scaffolds; whatever he will get from this will be in the indicative. He will never obtain a proposition that says: do this, or don't do that. . . . [89]

I am quoting Poincaré's statement because there exists an interesting contrast between his view and a recent work, a contrast that highlights the shift that has taken place since Poincaré's time regarding the scientific respectability of imperative, injunctive language forms. This shift is of importance to my subject, and the work in question is G. Spencer Brown's already mentioned book, *Laws of Form*.

Brown states:

Even natural science appears to be more dependent upon injunction than we are usually prepared to admit. The professional initiation of the man of science consists not so much in reading the proper textbooks, as in obeying injunctions such as "look down that microscope." But it is

Injunctive Language—Behavior Prescriptions

not out of order for men of science, having looked down the microscope, now to describe to each other, and to discuss amongst themselves, what they have seen, and to write papers and textbooks describing it. Similarly, it is not out of order for mathematicians, each having obeyed a given set of injunctions to describe to each other, and to discuss amongst themselves, what they have seen, and to write papers and textbooks describing it. But in each case, the description is dependent upon, and secondary to, the set of injunctions having been obeyed first. [17, p. 78]

And even more directly related to the essence of injunctions (behavior prescriptions) and their practical consequences is the following:

It may be helpful at this stage to realize that the primary form of mathematical communication is not description, but injunction. In this respect it is comparable with practical art forms like cookery, in which the taste of a cake, although literally indescribable can be conveyed to a reader in the form of a set of injunctions called a recipe. Music is a similar art form, the composer does not even attempt to describe the set of sounds he has in mind, much less the set of feelings occasioned through them, but writes down a set of commands which, if they are obeyed by the reader, can result in a reproduction, to the reader, of the composer's original experience [17, p. 77].

Thus, a command to do something—that is, a behavior prescription—has the potential of conveying to somebody the immediate experience and realization of certain reality aspects that could not be communicated by mere digital, analytical, verbal descriptions or explanations. How relevant all this is for our considerations becomes especially obvious if we recall Galin's statement (page 35) that the experience of attending a symphony concert cannot be readily expressed in words, while the concept "democracy requires informed participation" is difficult to convey in images.

131

We thus begin to realize that behavior prescriptions offer a third direct access to the right hemisphere, and with it, to a person's world image. And we also see that—like Monsieur Jourdain and his prose—we have always utilized injunctive language forms when we deliberately (or, more likely, outside of our awareness) tried to motivate the behavior of our clients towards certain goals.

Behavior prescriptions range from very simple, direct commands to highly complex combinations of therapeutic double binds, reframings, and illusions of alternatives. It will hardly surprise the reader to find that interventions of this kind cannot be stereotypically applied to similar cases, but that every case presupposes as comprehensive a consideration of all the elements of a situation—especially its interpersonal aspects—as possible and therefore requires a specific plan. This requires inventiveness and flexibility and confronts the therapist with ever new challenges, decisions, and responsibilities. Since my colleagues and I have presented this subject in greater detail in our book *Change* [117], and since the present book deals mostly with the use of language in psychotherapy, a few examples of different complexity may suffice.

In marriage therapy it happens quite frequently that one spouse does most of the talking and may even answer questions directed at the partner before the latter has a chance to deal with the question. This is usually done in a framework of supposed helpfulness and can therefore be difficult to deal with. Erickson may approach the problem in the following way:

When I ask a husband for his point of view and the wife interrupts even when I ask her not to, then I usually find some action that will quiet her. For example, I will do it this way. I say to the wife, "I still want your husband's point of view, and you keep right on talking. I know it is because of your eagerness to help me understand. But do you happen to have a lipstick?" Of course she usually has a lipstick, and I ask her to take it out of her purse. Then I say, "Now, this will seem ridiculous to you, but suppose you hold that lipstick like this"—I show her that I want her to hold it with the tip just gently touching her lips. "Now keep it right there, just touching. I'm going to ask your husband some questions, and I want you to notice how your lips want to move. I think you'll find it very interesting." A woman can get quite fascinated watching the quivering of her lips on that lipstick. By doing that, I've given her a legitimate use for her lips. She doesn't quite understand it, but she finds it amusing. [53, p. 227]

The next example shows the elegance of a seemingly minimal intervention into a human system whose rigid, monolithic structure was thereby changed rapidly and fundamentally. Erickson once treated a couple who were caught in a typical problem which he describes as follows:

This husband and wife had been running a restaurant business together for many years and they were in a constant quarrel about the management of it. The wife insisted that the husband should manage it, and he protested that she never let him do it. As he put it, "Yes, she keeps telling me I should run the restaurant. All the time she's running it she tells me I should do it. I'm the bus boy, I'm the janitor, I scrub the floors. She nags at me about the buying, she nags at me about the bookkeeping, she nags at me because the floor needs scrubbing."

She, on the other hand, claimed that she would only be too happy to let him manage the restaurant and have more time to be at home. Both were thus convinced that if they could not follow their individual preference (manage the restaurant and spend more time at home, respectively) it was the *other's* fault. Seen from *outside* the system both wishes were, of course, perfectly compatible. Seen from *within* the system they were not. This dyadic relationship was thus caught in what in communication theory is called a *game-without-end* [116, pp. 232–36] and which

133

comes about when a system is enmeshed in its own rigid rules and is unable to generate from within itself a rule for the change of its rules (that is, a metarule). Where this is the case, the metarule must be introduced from the outside and its selection and input into the system becomes the task of therapy. Usually this is attempted by means of interpretations, explanations, and occasional confrontations which seem to offer themselves as the most obvious intervention—first, because of the paramount, but to my mind unjustified, importance attributed to *insight* (that is, left-hemispheric understanding) as a *conditio sine qua non* of change; and secondly, because acting instead of talking is considered manipulative.

As always in such cases, Erickson first undertook that painstakingly detailed exploration of even the seemingly most insignificant elements of the situation and the couple's interaction which eventually enables him to direct his intervention at the crucial point of the problem, even though on superficial examination this point may appear quite trivial. He thus learned that the two opened their restaurant every morning at seven and closed it at ten in the evening. The wife had the keys, while he parked or fetched the car. Erickson gave them the following, apparently very simple behavior prescription: The husband was to get to the restaurant half an hour before she did. Since they only had one car, she had to walk several blocks to join him. But by the time she got to the restaurant, the situation was a very different one. Again in Erickson's words:

When the husband arrived a half hour before his wife, *he* carried the keys. *He* opened the door. *He* unlocked everything. *He* set up the restaurant for the day. When his wife arrived, she was completely out of step and way behind. So many things had been set in motion by him, and he was managing them.

Of course, when she remained behind at home that half hour in the morning, it left her with the breakfast dishes and the housework to do before she left. And if she could be a half hour late, she could be thirty-five minutes late. In fact, what she hadn't recognized when she agreed to the arrangement was that she could be forty minutes or even an hour late. In this way, she discovered that her husband could get along at the restaurant without her. Her husband, in turn, was discovering that he could manage the restaurant. [53, p. 226]

Once she found it all right to arrive late in the morning, she gradually began to leave early in the evening, preparing a bed-time snack for him. By bringing about this minimal change in their interaction—indeed, so minimal that the spouses did not offer a great deal of resistance—Erickson effected a decisive systemic change (a second-order solution that changed the structure of the system itself) and he achieved this by way of concrete action rather than by interpreting.

A graduate student comes into therapy. He has completed all the requirements for a doctoral degree except for completing and submitting his dissertation. The writing of the dissertation causes him unusual difficulties which he has not yet been able to resolve in spite of three years of hard work. It is January and the last, irre-vocable extension granted him by the university expires on 15 May. He is the pride of a large clan of poor immigrants who see in him, the future doctor, the justification of all their depriva-tions and the fulfillment of their own unfulfilled expectations. This produces in the young, very intelligent, and so far quite suc-cessful man an intense fear of failure which manifests itself in the following way: Whatever he does must be so perfect as not to offer any point of possible criticism. Regarding the dissertation, this means that he must anticipate in it every conceivable objection and must make reference to all the pertinent works by other au-thors. Whenever he does not feel completely safe or when a doubt arises in his mind, he adds a footnote, but in order to

135

phrase this footnote in the best way possible and just to be on the safe side, he decides to read yet another book in which he then typically finds additional material or arguments that he has not yet covered in his dissertation. The latter is thus growing into mastodontic proportions. In the three years he has written 400 pages, but they comprise only the first three of eight chapters. He realizes that if he continues in this way he will not be able to finish the work by the deadline. Every day he torments himself many hours at his desk or in the libraries and he apparently cannot shake off the impression that the members of his thesis committee are looking over his shoulder, just waiting for him to commit a mistake or an omission. At first, all interventions directed at his self-defeating *modus operandi* fail, until he is eventually given the instruction to expose himself several times to public ridicule in a harmless way until the next therapy session. As always with this type of short-therapeutic intervention, here, too, the goal of this behavior prescription was the attempted, but problem-perpetuating solution: His anxious avoidance of any mistake and ridicule that was the chief effect of his paralyzing perfectionism. The following report is transcribed from the sound-recording of the next session with him:

"The first time I did it, I went into a Mexican restaurant and insisted upon an egg roll* and asked: 'Isn't that Mexican food?' I felt terrible. I had to steel myself to enter the place and felt extremely embarrassed and self-conscious. The next time, on the street, walking down a street I knew, I asked where that street was—and I felt less embarrassed and I had to steel myself less. And as I asked those types of directions more and more, the easier and easier it got and—ah [pause] ah, I began to feel more and more how seriously I take myself and how silly it is [short laugh] and—ah, how this—I'm naturally a reflective person and consequently I began to speculate or connect all this to my problem and my personality and my life and my past and my childhood etc. etc.—but,

* A small, meat-filled pancake; a typical specialty of Chinese cuisine.

136

in effect, it's taking myself very seriously and I have lessened that. . . .
A very useful exercise [pause] I mean the results were quite immediate,
that is to say, I started taking myself less seriously and was a little less
concerned and less up-tight and constricted, worrying about projecting
an image or whatever. . . .*

Anxious anticipations or dreaded situations that are the core element of anxiety neuroses and phobias, always distinguish themselves by a high degree of absurdity and are for this reason beyond
the reach of reasonable arguments. But this very fact makes them
accessible to behavior prescriptions whose bizarre and illogical
nature run counter to commonsense. Of course, when utilizing
such interventions we must not only observe the rule of the
unresolved remnant, but we may find it necessary to approach
the goal in minimal steps and in very roundabout ways. The
phobic who cannot enter brightly lit, crowded buildings may gain
a measure of reassurance if instructed to enter the building but to
stop one yard short of the critical point at which his anxiety
would overwhelm him. From a reasonable, left-hemispheric
point of view this is absurd. What is it supposed to mean and
where exactly is that point? But in the subjective experience of
the phobic this injunctive communication has a very different effect: He now pushes a safety zone, one yard wide, ahead of him,
and the situation is thereby pragmatically reframed for him from
an absolute to a relative problem. Notice also that the intervention is based on a specific visualization. In essentially the same
way, Erickson once seemed to disregard completely the "real"
problem of a patient, his compulsion to take numerous showers,
and first merely told him to use a different kind of soap, then different towels, gradually changed the times of the showers and so
on, thus almost imperceptibly creating wider and wider cracks in
the apparently monolithic structure of this neurosis.

* In the follow-up interview some four months later, we learned that he had managed
to submit his dissertation in time and have it accepted.

9

Anything Except THAT

*Dal dire al fare
c'è di mezzo il mare.**

—Italian proverb

THE MOST FREQUENTLY stated doubt about the therapeutic techniques mentioned so far usually takes the form of the
question: How can one get reasonable people, capable of independent judgment, to carry out these unreasonable and often
quite inane actions? However, clinical experience shows that our
patients—especially those who are at their wit's end—will often
discern in the absurd, paradoxical nature of these injunctions the
possibility of a solution which they have so far not considered.
And the fact that these tasks are safe, that they seem comfortably
far removed from the "real" problem and require little time,
money, and energy additionally contributes to their acceptance
and execution.

* Between saying and doing there lies the ocean.

Anything Except THAT

Of course, this is by no means the rule. Every correctly designed prescription will—precisely because it "fits"—run up against the same resistance which has so far made it impossible for our clients to resolve their problems by themselves. It may be a useful simplification to postulate that whoever comes into therapy signals in one way or another: Anything, except *that*. By this I mean that emotional suffering creates a willingness to do *anything* for its alleviation, except one and only one thing; and this "one thing" is exactly what causes his suffering. With this *proviso* the sufferer closes the vicious circle of his problem and of the problem-perpetuating pseudosolution. The only possible solution always lies in the direction of the greatest anxiety and, therefore, the strongest resistance.

The question thus is how in the face of this "anything, except *that*" attitude we can find the way across the ocean which, according to the proverb mentioned above, separates the behavior prescription (the saying) from its practical execution (the doing). Again, there exists a number of possible interventions which shall now be described without any claim of completeness.

SPEAKING THE PATIENT'S "LANGUAGE"

One of the most basic differences between traditional psychotherapy and certain brief-therapeutic (including hypnotherapeutic) procedures is the fact that in the former the patient is first taught a new "language," the language of the theory his therapist subscribes to. This learning process is of necessity time-consuming and greatly contributes to the length of classic therapies.

Hypnosis, since time immemorial, utilizes a diametrically opposite approach: The hypnotist learns and employs the language of his client; the term *language* being meant here metaphorically and literally. In other words, the therapist not only does his utmost to arrive at an understanding of the client's values, expectations, hopes, fears, prejudices—in short, his world image—as quickly and as completely as possible, but he also pays attention to the *actual* language of his client and utilizes it in his own verbalizations. It should be immediately obvious that one must talk a different language with a child than with an adult, or with an uneducated person than with a cerebral academician. But over and above these differences, the semantics of a person reveals the sensory modalities with which he primarily perceives his world. It is known that some people are "visual types," while others experience life mostly proprioceptively. Less well known is the fact that these modalities express themselves in everyday language. "I simply cannot see why . . . ," "Only at that moment the scales fell from my eyes," "When it comes to that he has a real tunnel vision" obviously are related to a predominantly visual experience of reality, as are references to shapes and colors or the description of a person or a situation in almost photographic detail. "I have butterflies in my stomach," "He gives me a creepy feeling," "This just seems to stick in his throat" and countless other, similar statements are evidence of a world image that is primarily of a proprioceptive nature. If one learns to listen not only to the content but also to the style of communication, it becomes relatively easy to identify and utilize these modalities in therapeutic discourse. The interested reader is again referred to Bandler and Grinder's work [7, 8].

It should be immediately clear that this approach requires a significant change in a therapist's own stance. Instead of seeing himself as a firm rock in a sea of trouble, he becomes a chameleon. And it is at this point that many therapists themselves prefer to dig in behind the retort, "Anything, except *that*," while for others the necessity of ever new adaptations to the world images of their clients is a fascinating task.

This necessity to learn the language of the patient is virtually identical with what Viehweg (cf. footnote on page 42), in his reference to Aristotle's *Topica*, calls a *search for premises*. For this is indeed what we are doing: We search for premises and, having found them, utilize them as the vehicle of change. As Xenophon said of Socrates: "Whenever he wanted to explain something, he set out with premises that offered the greatest probability of agreement, holding this to be the only sure method of argument. Accordingly, whenever he argued, he gained greater assent than any man I have ever known" [123].

To exemplify this point, here is first of all a quite literal example of "learning the patient's language" which has the additional advantage of conveying an idea of the unusual linguistic ability and the perseverance of Milton Erickson.

Working as a young psychiatrist in a hospital, he came across an intriguing case. The patient was a man of approximately 25 years of age who had been picked up by the police for disturbed behavior. Since he had no documents and had never been reported missing, nobody knew who he was, and he had remained in the hospital ever since his admission. He himself offered no information or explanations, except for the three utterances "My name is George," "Good morning" and "Good night." To any attempt to enter into a conversation with him he reacted with lengthy, rapid verbalizations in a totally incomprehensible artifical language. Over the years numerous psychiatrists, psychologists, nurses, social workers, and fellow patients had attempted to make sense out of this word salad and to induce George to make himself understood. Erickson joined the hospital staff in the sixth year of George's stay, and he describes his intervention as follows:

A secretary recorded in shorthand the word-salads with which he so urgently greeted those who entered the ward. These transcribed recordings were studied but no meaning could be discovered. These word-salads were carefully paraphrased, using words that were least likely to be found in George's productions and an extensive study was made of these until the author could improvise a word-salad similar in pattern to George's, but utilizing a different vocabulary. . . .

The author then began the practice of sitting silently on the bench beside George daily for increasing lengths of time until the span of an hour was reached. Then, at the next sitting, the author, addressing the empty air, identified himself verbally. George made no response.

The next day the identification was addressed directly to George. He spat out an angry stretch of word-salad to which the author replied, in tones of courtesy and responsiveness, with an equal amount of his own carefully contrived word-salad. George appeared puzzled and when the author finished, George uttered another contribution with an inquiring intonation. As if replying the author verbalized still further word-salad.

After a half dozen interchanges, George lapsed into silence and the author promptly went about other matters.

The next morning appropriate greetings were exchanged employing proper names by both. Then George launched into a long word-salad speech to which the author courteously replied in kind. There followed then brief interchanges of long and short utterances of word-salad until George fell silent and the author went to other duties.

This continued for some time. Then George, after returning the morning greeting, made meaningless utterances without pause for four hours. It taxed the author greatly to miss lunch and to make a full reply in kind. George listened attentively and made a two-hour reply to which a weary two-hour response was made. (George was noted to watch the clock throughout the day.)

The next morning George returned the usual greeting properly but added about two sentences of nonsense to which the author replied with a similar length of nonsense. George replied, "Talk sense, Doctor." "Certainly, I'll be glad to. What is your last name?" "O'Donovan and it's about time somebody who knows how to talk asked. Over five years in this lousy joint" . . . (to which was added a sentence or two of word-salad). The author replied, "I'm glad to get your name, George. Five years is too long a time" . . . (and about two sentences of word-salad were added).

Within a year George's progress made possible his release. He found a job and Erickson reports that every once in a while he came back to pay a brief visit. Almost invariably he began or terminated the reports on his progress with a bit of word-salad, expecting the same from Dr. Erickson and adding: "Nothing like a little nonsense in life, is there, Doctor?" [28]

A somewhat less literal use of the patient's "language" was made in the case of the overprotective mother, mentioned on page 123. She was evidently unwilling to solve her son's problem in any way other than by her dedicated maternal help. Instead of committing the same mistake that everybody else before him had made by giving the obvious, commonsensical counsel to leave the boy alone and let him find his own way to deal with his problems, the therapist reframed the situation by demanding from her a particularly difficult form of help—the language of help being the only language she was willing to listen to. And in the fictitious example of the robber (page 118) the victim likewise utilizes the other's language. He does not, indeed cannot, try to change the context of threatened violence and of illegal appropriation of money, but proposes, in the *robber's "language,"* a different and much more enticing possibility.

Erickson once found himself confronted with a comparable threat. A severely depressed woman, leading a totally isolated life, told him in their first session that he was her last hope and gave him three months to help her. If the therapy did not help, she would then kill herself. Instead of trying the same or more of the same that others before him had already tried unsuccessfully—that is, to talk her out of her depression and her ideas of suicide—Dr. Erickson adopted her language: In one of his typical, long, monotonous monologues he cautiously (and, of course, without any sarcasm) recommended that she should use these three remaining months to enjoy all that which for years she would have liked to do, but either had not dared to or had not been able to afford. Since for many weeks she had not taken care of herself, was badly dressed, unkempt, and offered a sorry picture of general neglect, he proposed first of all that she should go to a beauty parlor and experience at least once in her life that which for more fortunate women is a weekly routine. In a similar vein and without any direct reference to her intended suicide he wondered if there was any reason why she should not spend all her money for the most tempting delicacies, for elegant clothes, and other luxury items that she had never dared to buy. The end of the story is not difficult to guess. By staying within the frame of her ultimatum and never questioning it, he succeeded in leading her, step by small step, out of this frame and changed her world image.

UTILIZING THE PATIENT'S RESISTANCE

In every conflict situation there are basically two ways of defending oneself against the opponent's thrusts: to react with a counter-thrust of at least equal force or to yield, thereby letting the other's attack fall into the void and making him lose his balance. The usefulness of this second, "Judo"-method in psychotherapy is recognized by many authors, and it is generally accepted that the utilization of resistance (for example, of negative transference phenomena) can have positive, therapeutic results. In actual fact, however, these considerations often exhaust themselves in lip service and resistance only too soon becomes a "sign that the patient is not yet ready for therapy." Here, too, a great deal can be learned from hypnotherapy where the ability to utilize resistance and to reframe any setback as a sign of progress has always been considered decisive for ultimate success.

To return once more to the anxious, overprotective mother (page 123), she successfully countered all requests to control herself and let her son sink or swim. The therapist utilized her resistance by not only *not* trying to make her desist from her overprotectiveness, but by demanding that she do *more of the same*. This request was unacceptable to her because it was defined as a necessary complication of her son's life and she could reject it only through doing *less of the same*. As mentioned already, this example shows that not only the utilization of (existing) resistance but also its provocation can enter into the service of therapy. To this end one reframes a situation in a way that to the client either seems absurd, inane, or for some other reason so incompatible with his world image that he has to reject the reframing, but in order to reject it has no alternative than doing precisely that which—unbeknownst to him—is behavior leading to the desired solution. A resistance is thus first provoked and then utilized.

Another example is provided by the specific pattern of interaction so frequently encountered in family psychotherapy between a rebellious teenager and his parents who are either at their wit's end or continue to try more of the same useless solution consisting in increased sanctions. In the presence of the teenager the therapist can usually reframe the situation by pompously invoking his "long clinical experience with cases of this kind" and asserting that the youngster is not really insolent, but is reacting to a deep-seated, existential fear of growing up and of losing the comfortable safety of childhood. This redefinition has a double purpose. First, it almost invariably mobilizes the teenager's resistance because the insinuation of fear is unacceptable to him; the way he sees himself and the situation, he acts from a position of strength and courage. But since for once he is not up against a prohibition or a command, but against the benevolent judgment of an expert about what "really" goes on inside himself, he can demolish this expert opinion only by proving that he is not a helpless pawn of uncontrollable anxiety. This proof, however, can only be given by behaving less rebelliously, while the therapist can define every new instance of insolent behavior as "proof" for the correctness of his diagnosis. Secondly, this intervention leads to a change in the parents' problem-perpetuating pseudosolution. For if they are at all willing to consider the possibility that the expert's depth-psychological explanation may be correct, they are likely to adopt at least some of that tolerant attitude that we are willing to grant people with deep-seated problems. On the one hand, this increased tolerance then makes it less necessary for the youngster to defy them, and on the other hand it forces him to prove to them even more clearly that it is not true that he is "compelled" to be insolent.

The next example gives an idea of the complexity into which an accomplished expert in the language of change can interweave the utilization of resistance with an illusion of alternatives and the multi-level logic of injunctive communication.

One evening Erickson's 8-year-old son Lal declared that from now on his father could no longer command him to do anything, and to prove it he would not eat his dinner. Erickson accepted the challenge but mentioned that it would be regrettable if Lal had to forego his dinner. Would drinking or refusing to drink a glass of milk decide the issue? The boy agreed. After dinner his father placed a large glass of milk on the table and the carefully planned ritual took its course. The first thing he told the child was: "Lal, drink your milk," and the latter answered with quiet determination: "I don't have to and you can't make me." After insisting several times, Erickson suddenly commanded: "Lal, spill your milk." The boy looked startled but quickly also refused this injunction. This interaction, too, was repeated several times. Next Lal was told to throw the glass on the floor and, of course, he refused. The father's next command was: "Don't pick up your glass of milk," and he defiantly lifted the glass. Immediately he was told: "Don't put your glass down," and he quickly placed it back on the table. Now the crucial part of the interaction followed and is repeated here in Dr. Erickson's own words:

Stepping over to the wall blackboard the father wrote "Lift your milk" at one end and at the other he wrote, "Put your milk down." He then explained that he would keep tally of each time Lal did something he had been told to do. He was reminded that he had already been told to do both of those things repeatedly, but that tally would now be kept by making a chalk mark each time he did either one of those two things he had been previously instructed to perform.

Lal listened with desperate attention.

The father continued, "Lal, don't pick up your glass," and made a tally mark under "Lift your milk" which Lal did in defiance. Then, "Don't put your milk down" and a tally mark was placed under, "Put your milk down" when this was done. After a few repetitions of this, while Lal watched the increasing size of the score for each task, his father wrote on the blackboard, "Drink your milk" and "Don't drink your milk," explaining that a new score would be kept on these items.

Lal listened attentively but with an expression of beginning hopelessness.

Gently he was told, "Don't drink your milk now." Slowly he put the glass to his lips but before he could sip, he was told, "Drink your milk." Relievedly he put the glass down. Two tally marks were made, one under "Put your milk down," and one under, "Don't drink your milk."

After a few rounds of this, Lal was told not to hold his glass of milk over his head but to spill it on the floor. Slowly, carefully he held it at arm's length over his head. He was promptly admonished not to keep it there. Then the father walked into the other room, returned with a book and another glass of milk and remarked, "I think this whole thing is silly. Don't put your milk down."

With a sign of relief Lal put the glass on the table, looking at the scores on the blackboard, sighed again, and said, "Let's quit, Daddy."

"Certainly, Lal. It's a silly game and not real fun and the next time we get into an argument, let's make it really something important that we can both think about and talk sensibly about."

Lal nodded his head in agreement.

Picking up his book, the father drained the second glass of milk preparatory to leaving the room. Lal watched, silently picked up his glass and drained it. [30, pp. 148–50]

As the reader will appreciate, what is extraordinary about this example is not only the complex combination of different interventions but also the cautious way in which the father enabled his child to save face.

Sometimes the source of resistance lies not so much in the client himself as in his significant others and yet can be utilized or at least neutralized in very similar ways. An attractive, intelligent 21-year-old girl comes into therapy to seek a solution for her repeated failures in establishing and maintaining relationships with men. Her greatest wish is to marry soon and it seems that she therefore moves into any new encounter with such ill-concealed nubile enthusiasm that almost invariably the man in question quickly disappears over the horizon. For her it is incomprehensible why these men never call back and ask her out again, except that she has jumped to the conclusion that there must be something very wrong with her. The situation is complicated by the fact that her father, who is himself a therapist and lives in a city several hundred miles away, is also very anxious to see her get married. It is his daily habit to call her, to make detailed inquiries about any "progress" in her private life and to heap well-meant advice on her. As can be imagined, these calls intensify the girl's self-defeating *modus operandi* and every "lost" day (crowned by the paternal telephone call) thus contributes to her near-panic. To bring about a first change in this problem-perpetuating behavior, it appears imperative to neutralize the father's incessant "help." This the girl seems incapable of achieving by herself for, after all, he is not only her father but, being a therapist, he of course knows exactly what she should do. He has read our book *Change* and it was he who told her to come and see us: "If anybody can help you, then those people in Palo Alto can." This apparent complication provides a useful avenue of approach. In the first session the girl is told to call her father and to report that for the time being we have forbidden her to tell him anything about the therapy and her private life, and further-more, that on the strength of his knowledge of our book he will know exactly why we are demanding this of her and why he must not explain to her our reason. Being thus promoted to co-therapist, the father has to stop his inquiries, which leads to an al-most immediate lessening of the girl's frantic quest, since at least she need no longer dread the daily telephone confessions of hav-ing "wasted" another day and the treatment thus can start on a much more relaxed note.

Almost the opposite situation exists in the relatively frequent cases in which progress in therapy is reported by third persons (spouses, parents, teachers, probation officers, physicians, social workers) whereas the patient himself insists that the treatment is not helping him in the least. The method of choice here is to in-struct him, without explaining the reason, that he must not under any circumstances report even the slightest improvement but rather, no matter what therapeutic effects he may notice, to report only that nothing has changed. Regardless of whether he accepts or rejects this behavior prescription, the therapist can now praise him for his willing cooperation every time he complains about the lack of progress—and especially when he insists that there *really* is no progress and that he is *really* complaining about it (and not because the therapist, for some absurd reason of his own, wants him to complain), also this complaint can be reframed as a particularly conscientious and imaginative compliance with the behavior prescription. What is involved here is the technique, mentioned already in the sections on reframing and on the illusion of alternatives, of setting a frame: The patient emphasizes that his complaint is to be understood as standing *outside* the frame of the therapist's injunction; the latter includes it *in* the frame by defining the statement: "My complaint is not in compliance with your command, but a real complaint" as being itself again an act of compliance with the command. The structure of this intervention is that of a Russellian paradox, for it rests on the difference between, or rather the confusion of, a logical class (complaining) with one of its members (one specific complaint). And finally this intervention also utilizes the technique of preempting, to be mentioned next.

PREEMPTING

In his *Rhetorica ad Alexandrum* [Rhetoric for Alexander] Aristotle refers to the technique of anticipating resistance as:

the method by which we shall counteract the ill-feeling which is experienced against us by anticipating the adverse criticisms of our audience and the arguments of those who are going to speak against us. . . . In matters then which are likely to annoy your listeners you must by anticipations of this kind bring forward reasons which will show that you are justified in offering advice. . . . [3, p. 18]

The anticipation thus *preempts* the resistance and in this effect lies its usefulness for therapeutic communication. A few examples shall illustrate this:

"You will probably find this silly, but I have the impression that . . ."

"This is bound to sound ridiculous, but one could say . . ."

"There exists a relatively simple solution for this problem, but I am almost sure that you will not like it."

"I know that few people would look at the situation in this way, but . . ."

"To do this will be very difficult for you, because on the surface this solution is likely to look quite absurd."

Preempting thus almost demands agreement by implying that disagreement would be a sign of limited understanding, lack of imagination or courage, or an otherwise mediocre mind.

A close derivative of preempting—and also of the confusion technique—are formulations through which one says something by claiming that one does not (or would not) say it. This, too, was already known to Aristotle, who recommended:

. . . say something and pretend that you are not saying it. . . . Such is the way briefly to remind your listeners of something under the pretense of omitting it. [3, p. 21]

It may be assumed that this odd form of communication is effective because the absurdity of stating that which is allegedly not stated blocks the left hemisphere, while the right, with its notorious inability to process negations, receives the statement in its intended meaning. Some practical examples are:

"If your wife were not here, I would say the following: . . ."

"If I were not your therapist, I would simply point out that . . ."

"Somebody less desperate than you I would probably tell quite frankly that I consider this problem rather trivial."

"The trouble with the two of you is that you are very intelligent people—and therefore a relatively unimportant situation can appear very critical to you."

Let me conclude with some general remarks about the wide and fertile field of behavior prescriptions and the resistance against them. As already mentioned, for obvious technical reasons any therapeutic injunction, behavior prescription, or homework assignment must be acceptable (that is, compatible with our client's world image), must be safe and reasonably easy to perform, inexpensive, apparently quite removed from the "real" problem, and, above all, not degrading—although this need not exclude actions that appeal to a client's sense of the absurd. Simple, seemingly insignificant prescriptions are usually more effective than complicated ones that leave too much room for misunderstanding and error; and those that require a certain *action* are more reliable than others that consist merely in a verbalization (for example, "I want you to go home and tell your husband . . . "). Furthermore, the patient is always right (except that he could perhaps be even righter than he thinks), and the therapist never enters into open contest with him. If a client refuses to accept a behavior prescription or first accepts it but then does not carry it out, it is useful to take full responsibility for this failure and to apologize for having been carried away by therapeutic enthusiasm and to have imposed on the client more than the latter is willing and capable of accepting. It is then often possible to give him a basically identical injunction under a somewhat different guise and in different words.

Needless to say, the finding of the appropriate and acceptable intervention is no easy task. Rossi uses the analogy of "a mental locksmith now gently trying this key and now that" [30, p. 151].

The mistake most frequently committed by novices consists in forcing a behavior prescription into a single sentence and then to be discouraged if the patient either completely misunderstands or ignores it. Here, too, training in hypnotherapy is a great asset: Any suggestion, including those given to a subject in a nontrance state—which is what a behavior prescription essentially amounts to—must be given in slow, clear, and repetitive language; a language that anticipates all possible misunderstandings and closes all loopholes. In general discourse we are all loath to repeat a certain point too often, as this appears to cast aspersion on our partner's intelligence. In therapeutic communication, however, we are only too often surprised to find that, having made one and the same point over and over again and repeating it once more with trepidation, our patient may suddenly say: "That is really true—why have you never told me that before?"

With regards to the slow, repetitive language of suggestion, the so-called *shingles technique* can be taken over from hypnosis into general psychotherapy. It consists in making the second half of every sentence into the first half of the next one and is thus similar to the way roof shingles are placed so that one row half overlaps the other. An example taken from a typical induction may illustrate this verbal style:

"I shall now slowly count from one to five. When I get to five I shall slightly tap the table. When you hear this slight tap, you will notice a sensation of relaxed comfort in your body. As soon as you notice this feeling of relaxation . . ."

10

Therapeutic Rituals

LET US SUPPOSE that Dr. Erickson had told the patient, mentioned on page 62, to go home and to *actually* defrost her refrigerator. With this behavior prescription he would have extended the symbolic, imaginary nature of his intervention from his patient's second-order into her first-order reality—that is, the *real* refrigerator, its *real* defrosting, and so on. This would then have been a sequence of behaviors, combining symbolic and concrete elements, to which the term *ritual* would be fully applicable.

Ritual is the most comprehensive and the most elegant synthesis of all the interventions and techniques mentioned in this book. The archetypical role and function of ritual all over the world and in all periods of history and prehistory is well known, and the literature on this subject is vast. "If mankind were to become extinct save for one fairly gifted child that has not received any education whatsoever, this child would rediscover the entire course of events, would re-create gods, demons, paradise, commandments and prohibitions, old and new testaments, everything," writes Hermann Hesse in *Demian*.

It is probably one of the basic illnesses of modern time that in our left-hemispheric *hubris* we have banished ritual from our lives. For while we apparently succeeded in performing this excision, the age-old longing for the mystery of rituals remains unfulfilled and either contributes to an acute feeling of senselessness and emptiness, or attaches itself to such pitiful substitutes as the acquisition of a driver's license instead of a rite of initiation. Admittedly, there still exist rituals, such as the Brazilian carnival, but many have become empty vessels, such as its European counterpart, the *Fasching*, or modern marriage ceremonies. Ritual has largely been forced into the underground and thus has greatly restricted the contribution of the right hemisphere to the solution of concrete problems, or else threatens the reasonable order of the world by the dark, orphic violence which is typical of the repressed. How many people would find it easier and less painful to overcome the breakdown of their marriage if the banal signing of the divorce papers were embedded into some modern ritual? And only dictators and similar riff-raff seem to be aware of this deep need and rarely fail to offer the younger generation those pseudorituals that will serve their nefarious ends.

More than others it was C. G. Jung who emphasized the psychotherapeutic importance of ritual throughout his work, but he, too, saw it predominantly as a "one-way street" and limited himself to the exploration and analysis of mankind's ancient rituals or of those which manifest themselves spontaneously in individual dreams, fantasies, and delusions—that is, to their translation into the language of the left hemisphere. Typical for this perspective is Plaut's recent article with the suggestive title "Where Have All the Rituals Gone?" [87] in which he examines their role in our modern world, but again in terms of a one-way translation. But when Madame Sechehaye [101] offers an apple to her catatonic patient Renée, or when John Rosen [94] actively enters into the delusional world of his patients, ritual is transformed from a spontaneous phenomenon into a planned, active intervention.

To the best of my knowledge it was the psychiatrist Mara Selvini and her collaborators at the *Istituto per lo Studio della Famiglia* in Milan who introduced the technique of deliberate, well-planned rituals into interactional psychotherapy. According to Dr. Selvini,

. . . a family ritual is an action, or a series of actions, accompanied by verbal formulae and involving the entire family. Like every ritual it must consist of a regular sequence of steps taken at the right time and at the right place [102, p. 238]

And further:

The "invention" of a family ritual invariably calls for a great creative effort on the part of the therapist and often, if I may say so, for flashes of genius, if only because a ritual that has proved effective in one family is unlikely to prove equally effective in another. This is because every family follows special *rules* and plays special *games*. In particular, *a ritual is not a form of metacommunication about these rules, let alone about these games; rather it is a kind of counter-game* which, once played, destroys the original game. In other words, it leads to the replacement of an unhealthy and epistemologically false rite (for example, the anorexic symptom) by one that is healthy and epistemologically sound. [102, p. 239]

As this last quotation shows, for Selvini the communication patterns of disturbed families are themselves rituals—but of course pathogenic ones. This suggests the applicability of the maxim *similia similibus curantur*. One of her case descriptions is quoted here in its entirety, also because it is such an unusually clear description of a particular pattern of pathological interaction:

Therapeutic Rituals

The child, whose EEG had shown minimal brain damage, was brought to family therapy when a child psychoanalyst refused to continue his treatment. The child seemed totally inaccessible to psychoanalytic approaches and, moreover, intolerably hostile. After four sessions with the parents, two in the presence of the child, the therapists realized that, apart from being exposed to intense interparental conflicts, the child had been forced into a double bind situation from which he could not extricate himself. Labelled "sick" by the neurologists and having been doctored with massive doses of sedatives, he was treated like a maniac at home and hence allowed to behave in a way that no parents would have taken from normal children: vicious kicks at the mother's face as she bent down to tie his shoelaces; lunges with the table-knife; plates of soup over his mother's dress, etc. By contrast he was invariably treated to long sermons and reproaches about his past misdeeds whenever he behaved like a normal child of his age. The therapists saw quickly that their first move must be the eradication of this double bind situation, and this by destroying the parents' conviction that their child was "mental." But they also realized that they could not achieve this end by verbal explanations, which would have been disqualified there and then. Instead they decided to prescribe the following family ritual: that same evening, after supper, the entire family, consisting of the father, the mother, the patient, his little sister and the maternal grandmother, would go in procession to the bathroom, the father carrying all the child's medicine bottles and solemnly addressing the following words to his son: "Today we were told by the doctors that we must throw all these medicines away because you are perfectly well. All you are is a naughty child, and we simply won't take any more of your nonsense." Thereupon he would pour the contents of the bottles, one by one and with great ceremony down the lavatory, all the time repeating: "You are perfectly well." This ritual proved so effective (notwithstanding the mother's fears that the child would kill her without his sedatives) that it led to the disappearance of the aggressive behavior and soon afterwards, to an amicable solution of the secret interparental conflicts (ten sessions).[102, pp. 236–37]

There is no doubt that further developments and refinements of therapeutic rituals will lend added effectiveness to family and other forms of interactional therapy.

11

Conclusion

THE UNORTHODOX NATURE of the techniques described here, especially their nonpsychological rationale, usually raises three skeptical questions:

The first has to do with the choice of the specific interventions. The criteria of their selection appear to have been left completely aside in this book and thus seem to be pulled out of the thin air. Of the overwhelmingly large number of possible or even imaginable interventions, how shall a therapist decide which one is indicated in any given case? The answer is trivially simple and therefore contributes to further skepticism: By carefully exploring what the clients have so far done in order to solve their problem. If, instead of engaging in the time-honored but futile exercise of exploring anamnestically *why* a human system came to behave the way it behaves, we decide to investigate *how* it behaves *here and now* and what the consequences of this behavior are, we shall find that the actual problem is what the system has so far tried to do in order to solve its supposed problem, and it is then obvious that the therapeutic intervention must be directed at this repeated, problem-engendering pseudosolution. *The solution is the problem* [117, pp. 31–39] and it alone, therefore, determines the nature and the structure of the intervention.

The second objection refers to the length of effectiveness of these interventions and is a *curiosum sui generis*. In virtually no other, comparable realm of human endeavor is it postulated and accepted that changes must be final and complete. Everywhere, except in classical psychotherapy, it is considered a simple fact of life that there are no perfect solutions, to be reached once and for all, that problems can recur and that existence is a life-long process of perhaps optimal, but certainly never perfect adaptation—and be this only because the scenario of life constantly changes. In therapy, however, we talk about such wondrous states as full genital organization, individuation, and self-actualization, and we consider a treatment to have been successful only if the difficulty or the symptom *never* occurs again. In this perspective the goal of therapy becomes the achievement of a utopian state of freedom from suffering and problems, while the reaching of the "mere" ability to live with one's pain and to cope with problems when and as they arise is considered a superficial palliative.* It would go well beyond the scope of this work to expose the extremely negative effects that necessarily follow from this utopia in relation to the length and the effectiveness of psychotherapeutic treatment, and how they are intimately connected with the unproven dogma that the elucidation of the causes in the past is an indispensable precondition for the change of their consequences in the present. But the patient, for instance, who could not say "no" and therefore tried to avoid de-

---

* "I do not treat, I analyze," one of my teachers was wont to say proudly, and he emptied the vessel of his scorn over the warning example of a colleague who had somehow managed to get a patient over his symptom in 45 minutes.

nials, knew the genesis of her symptom—and what did help her was not this knowledge, but the effect of the therapeutic double bind imposed on her here and now. The rebellious teenager who stopped his disruptive behavior in juvenile hall did, of course, not suddenly turn into an angel and kept posing difficult disciplinary problems which kept requiring imaginative solutions. The aim of realistic, responsible therapy can only be an increased skill in dealing with life problems as they arise, but not a problem-free life.

The third objection aims at the seeming superficiality of this approach, which so patently contradicts the belief that human problems are deep-seated and for this reason require deep-reaching and lengthy procedures for their resolution. But the mere fact that a given technique does not fit into the conceptual framework of another theory cannot be taken as *a priori* evidence for the wrongness or uselessness of that technique. At the beginning of this book I mentioned that its thesis is simple but its application is not. The crucial point remains its practical application—but not in the sense of the old joke: *There is no such thing as piano playing; I have myself tried it several times and nothing came of it.*

Works Cited

1. Adler, Alfred. *The Practice and Theory of Individual Psychology*. New York: Harcourt, Brace, 1927.

2. Aristotle. *Nichomachean Ethics*.

3. ———. *Rhetorica ad Alexandrum* [Rhetoric for Alexander].

4. ———. *Topica* [Topics].

5. Arnim, Bettina von. *Goethes Briefwechsel mit einem Kinde* [Goethe's Correspondence with a Child]. Edited by Gustav Konrad. Frechen: Bartmann-Verlag, 1960, p. 271. As quoted by Bettelheim (13, p. 153).

6. Bakan, Paul. "The Right Brain Is the Dreamer." *Psychology Today*, November 1976, pp. 66–68.

7. Bandler, Richard, and Grinder, John. *The Structure of Magic, I. A Book about Language and Therapy*. Palo Alto: Science and Behavior Books, 1975. Cf. also *The Structure of Magic, II. A Book about Communication and Change*. Palo Alto: Science and Behavior Books, 1976.

8. ———. *Patterns of the Hypnotic Techniques of Milton H. Erickson, M.D.* Cupertino: Meta Publications, 1975.

9. Bateson, Gregory. *Steps to an Ecology of Mind*. New York: Ballantine Books, 1972, pp. 279–308.

10. ———; Jackson, Don. D.; Haley, Jay; and Weakland, John H. "Toward a Theory of Schizophrenia." *Behavioral Science* 1 (1956): 251–64.

11. Bausani, Alessandro. *Geheim- und Universalsprachen. Entwicklung und Typologie* [Secret and Universal Languages. Development and Typology.]. Stuttgart: W. Kohlhammer, 1970.

12. Berger, Peter L., and Luckman, Thomas. *The Social Construction of Reality*. New York: Doubleday, 1966.

13. Bettelheim, Bruno. *The Uses of Enchantment*. New York: Alfred A. Knopf, 1976, p. 6.

14. Bever, Thomas G., and Chiarello, Robert. "Cerebral Dominance in Musicians and Nonmusicians." *Science* 185 (1974): 537–39.

15. Bogen, Joseph E. "The Other Side of the Brain, II: An Appositional Mind." *Bulletin of the Los Angeles Neurological Society* 34 (1969): 135–62.

16. Boulding, Kenneth E. *The Image. Knowledge in Life and Science*. Ann Arbor: University of Michigan Press, 1956.

17. Brown, George S. *Laws of Form*. New York: Bantam Books, 1973.

18. Chuang Tzu. *Musings of a Chinese Mystic. Selections from the Philosophy of*

Chuang Tzu. With an introduction by Lionel Giles. London: John Murray, 1920, pp. 75–76.

19. Darboux, Gaston. *Eloge historique d' Henri Poincaré* [Historic Eulogy for Henri Poincaré]. Paris: Gauthier-Villars, 1913. As quoted in *The World of Mathematics*, James R. Newman, ed. New York: Simon and Schuster, 1956, p. 1375.

20. Dewson, James H. "Inside Every Monkey Sits a Little Bit of Man." *The Stanford Magazine* 4 (1976), pp. 50–54.

21. Dimond, Stuart. *The Double Brain*. Baltimore: Williams & Wilkins, 1972.

22. Domhoff, G. William. "But Why Did They Sit on the King's Right in the First Place?" *Psychoanalytic Review* 56 (1969–1970): 596.

23. Eccles, John C. *The Understanding of the Brain*. New York: McGraw-Hill, 1973.

24. Enzensberger, Hans Magnus. *The Consciousness Industry*. New York: Seabury Press, 1974, p. 15.

25. Erickson, Milton H. "Deep Hypnosis and Its Induction." In *Experimental Hypnosis*, Leslie M. LeCron, ed. New York: Macmillan, 1952, pp. 70–114. Reprinted in Haley (**54**, pp. 7–31).

26. ———. "Further Techniques of Hypnosis. Utilization Techniques." *American Journal of Clinical Hypnosis* 2 (1959): 3–21. Reprinted in Haley (**54**, p. 33).

27. ———. "The Confusion Technique in Hypnosis." *American Journal of Clinical Hypnosis* 6 (1964): 183–207. Reprinted in (**54**, pp. 130–57).

28. ———. "The Use of Symptoms as an Integral Part of Hypnotherapy." *American Journal of Clinical Hypnosis* 8 (1965): 57–65. Reprinted in (**54**, pp. 501–2).

29. ———. "The Interspersal Technique for Symptom Correction and Pain Control." *American Journal of Clinical Hypnosis* 3 (1966): 198–209. Reprinted in Haley (**54**, pp. 510–20).

30. ———, and Rossi, Ernest L. "Varieties of Double Bind." *American Journal of Clinical Hypnosis* 17 (1975): 143–57.

31. ———; Rossi, Ernest L.; and Rossi, Sheila I. *Hypnotic Realities. The Induction of Clinical Hypnosis and Forms of Indirect Suggestion*. With a foreword by André M. Weitzenhoffer. New York: Irvington Publishers, 1976.

32. Evans, J. Martin. *America: The View from Europe*. Stanford: The Portable Stanford, Stanford Alumni Association, 1976, pp. 47–48.

33. Farb, Peter, *Word Play, What Happens When People Talk*. New York: Alfred A. Knopf, 1974, p. 222.

34. Foerster, Heinz von. "On Constructing a Reality." In *Environmental Design Research*, vol. 2, W. F. E. Preiser, ed. Stroudsberg: Dowden, Hutchinson & Ross, 1973, pp. 35–46.

35. ———. "Notes pour une épistemologie des objets vivants" [Notes on an epistemology of living things]. In *L' unité de l' homme* [The Unity of Man], Edgar Morin and Massimo Piatelli-Palmarini, eds. Paris: Éditions du Seuil, 1974, pp. 401–07. English version: "Notes on an Epistemology of Living Things." Urbana: University of Illinois, Biological Computer Laboratory, publication no. 224.

36. Frankl, Viktor E. *The Doctor and the Soul*. New York: Alfred A. Knopf, 1957.

37. ———. "Paradoxical Intention." *American Journal of Psychotherapy* 14 (1960): 520–35.

38. Freud, Sigmund. *Jokes and Their Relation to the Unconscious*. Standard Edition, vol. 8 London: Hogarth Press, 1960.

39. ———. *New Introductory Lectures on Psycho-Analysis*. Standard Edition, vol. 22, p. 174. London: Hogarth Press, 1964.

67. Kekulé, August. As quoted by F. R. Japp, "Kekulé Memorial Lecture." *Journal of the Chemical Society* 73 (1893) 97–100.

Works Cited

41. ———, and Allen, Melanie. *Make 'em Laugh. Life Studies of Comedy Writers.* Palo Alto: Science and Behavior Books, 1975.

42. Galin, David. "Implications for Psychiatry of Left and Right Cerebral Specialization: A Neurophysiological Context for Unconscious Processes." *Archives of General Psychiatry* 31 (1974): 572–83.

43. Gauger, Hans-Martin. *Sprachbewusstsein und Sprachwissenschaft* [Language Consciousness and Linguistics]. Munich: R. Piper, 1976, p. 156.

44. Gazzaniga, Michael S. *The Bisected Brain.* New York: Appleton-Century-Crofts, 1970.

45. ———. "Changing Hemisphere Dominance by Changing Reward Probabilities in Split-Brain Monkeys." *Experimental Neurology* 33 (1971): 412–19.

46. ———. "One Brain—Two Minds?" *American Scientist* 60 (1972): 311–17.

47. Geschwind, Norman. "Studies of Hemispheric Connection." In *Brain Mechanisms Underlying Speech and Language,* Clark H. Millikan and Frederic Darley, eds. New York: Grune & Stratton, 1967.

48. Giono, Jean. *The Domenici Affair.* London: Museum Press, 1956.

49. Gombrich, Ernst H. *The Story of Art.* New York: Phaidon, 1950, p. 25.

50. Gombrich, Richard. "The Consecration of a Buddhist Image." *Journal of Asian Studies* 26 (1966): 23–26.

51. Gordon, Harold W. "Hemispheric Activity and Musical Performance." *Science* 189 (1974): 68–69.

52. ———, and Sperry, Roger W. "Olfaction following Surgical Disconnection of the Hemispheres in Man." Unpublished paper read at the annual convention of the Psychonomic Society, St. Louis, October 1968.

53. Haley, Jay. *Uncommon Therapy. The Psychiatric Techniques of Milton H. Erickson, M.D.* New York: W. W. Norton, 1973.

54. Haley, Jay, ed. *Advanced Techniques of Hypnosis and Therapy. Selected Papers of Milton H. Erickson, M.D.* New York: W. W. Norton, 1967.

55. Hilgard, Ernest R., and Hilgard, Josephine R. *Hypnosis in the Relief of Pain.* Los Altos: William Kaufman, 1975, pp. 86–102.

56. Hofmannsthal, Hugo von. *The Difficult Man.* In *Play and Libretti.* New York: Pantheon Books, Bollingen Series 33:3, 1963, pp. 712–13.

57. Holton, Gerald. Personal communication.

58. Hoppe, Klaus D. "Die Trennung der Gehirnhälften" [The Separation of the Cerebral Hemispheres]. *Psyche* 29 (1975): 919–40.

59. Hunter, John. *A Treatise on the Veneral Disease.* London: self-published, 1786, pp. 200–04.

60. Huxley, Aldous. *The Perennial Philosophy.* New York: Harper Brothers, 1944, p. 41.

61. Janet, Pierre. *Les névroses* [The Neuroses]. Paris: Bibliothèque de Philosophie, 1909.

62. Jaspers, Karl. *Von der Wahrheit* [On Truth]. Munich: R. Piper, 1947.

63. Jaynes, Julian. As quoted in *Science News* 108 (December 13, 1975): 378–83.

64. Jespersen, Otto. *Language, Its Nature, Development and Origin.* London: Allen & Unwin, 1922, p. 184.

65. Jung, Carl G. *Psychological Types.* New York: Harcourt, Brace, 1926.

66. Kafka, Franz. *Paradoxes and Parables.* New York: Schocken Books, 1935, pp. 15-17. Copyright © 1946, 1947, 1948, 1953, 1954, 1958 by Schocken Books Inc. Copyright © renewed 1974 by Schocken Books Inc. Reprinted by permission.

67. Kekulé, August. As quoted by F. R. Japp, "Kekulé Memorial Lecture." *Journal of the Chemical Society* 73 (1893) 97–100.

68. Kelly, George A. *The Psychology of Personal Constructs.* 2 vols. New York: W. W. Norton, 1955.

69. Kimura, Doreen. "The Asymmetry of the Human Brain." *Scientific American* 228 (1973): 70–78.

70. Kinsbourne, Marcel, and Smith, W. *Hemispheric Disconnections and Cerebral Function.* Springfield: Charles C. Thomas, 1974.

71. Koestler, Arthur. *The Act of Creation.* New York: Macmillan, 1964.

72. Kopperschmidt, Josef. *Allgemeine Rhetorik. Einführung in die Theorie der persuasiven Kommunikation* [General Rhetoric. Introduction to the Theory of Persuasive Communication]. Stuttgart: W. Kohlhammer, 1973.

73. Kuhn, Thomas S. *The Structure of Scientific Revolutions.* 2nd ed. Chicago: University of Chicago Press, 1970, p. 122.

74. Laing, Ronald D. "Mystification, Confusion, and Conflict." In *Intensive Family Therapy: Theoretical and Practical Aspects*, Ivan Boszormenyi-Nagy and James L. Framo, eds. New York: Harper & Row, 1965, pp. 349–50.

75. ———, and Esterson, Aaron. *Sanity, Madness, and the Family.* vol. 1, *Families of Schizophrenics.* London: Tavistock, 1964, p. 145.

76. Levy, Jerre. "Cerebral Asymmetries as Manifested in Split-Brain Man." In Kinsbourne and Smith (70, pp. 165–83).

77. Mally, Ernst. *Grundgesetze des Sollens. Elemente der Logik des Willens.* [Basic Laws of Commands. Elements of Deontic Logic.]. Graz: Leuscher & Lubensky, 1926, p. 36.

78. Mann, Thomas. *Mario and the Magician.* In *Stories of Three Decades.* New York: Alfred A. Knopf, 1936, pp. 532–51, passim.

79. Mauthe, Jörg. *Nachdenkbuch für Österreicher, insbesondere Austrophile, Austromasochisten und andere Austriaken* [A Book of Contemplations for Austrians, especially Austrophiles, Austromasochists and Other Austriaks]. Vienna: Molden, 1975, p. 20.

80. Muir, Kenneth. "The Uncomic Pun." *The Cambridge Journal* 3 (1949–1950): 472–85.

81. Noyes, Russell, and Kletti, Roy. "Depersonalization in the Face of Life-Threatening Danger: A Description." *Psychiatry* 39 (1976): 19–27.

82. O'Neill, John. *Prodigal Genius. The Life of Nikola Tesla.* New York: Yves Washburn, 1944.

83. Piaget, Jean. *The Construction of Reality in the Child.* New York: Basic Books, 1954.

84. Pierce, John R. *Symbols, Signal and Noise.* New York: Harper Brothers, 1961, p. 119.

85. Plato. *Gorgias*, 456–57.

86. ———. *The Republic.*

87. Plaut, A. "Where Have All the Rituals Gone?" *Journal of Analytical Psychology* 20 (1975): 3–17.

88. Plutarch. As quoted in Hermann Diels, *Fragmente der Vorsokratiker.* [Fragments of the Pre-Socratics]. 2nd ed., vol. 2. Berlin: Weidmann, 1907, p. 590.

89. Poincaré, Henri. *La morale et la science* [Morals and Science]. In *Dernières Pensées* [Last Thoughts]. Paris: Flammarion, 1913, p. 225.

90. Popper, Sir Karl Raimund. *Conjectures and Refutations: The Growth of Scientific Knowledge.* New York: Basic Books, 1962.

Works Cited

91. "Psychophysiological Aspects of Cancer." *Annals of the New York Academy of Sciences* 164 (1969): 307–634.

92. Quintilian, Marcus Fabius. *Institutio Oratoria* [The Training of an Orator]. Book XI, III/5.

93. Rescher, Nicholas. *The Logic of Commands.* New York: Dover, 1966.

94. Rosen, John N. *Direct Analysis. Selected Papers.* New York: Grune & Stratton, 1953.

95. Sacerdote, Paul. *"The Uses of Hypnosis in Cancer Patients."* In "Psychophysiological Aspects of Cancer." *Annals of the New York Academy of Sciences* 125 (1966): 1011–19.

96. Salimbene. *La bizarra cronaca di Frate Salimbene* [The Bizarre Chronicle of Brother Salimbene]. Lanciano: Carabba, 1926.

97. Schmidt, Arno. *Orpheus.* Frankfurt: M. Fischer, 1970, pp. 17 and 19.

98. Schneider, Wolf. *Wörter machen Leute. Magie und Macht der Sprache* [Words Make People. The Magic and Power of Language]. Munich: R. Piper, 1976.

99. Schrödinger, Erwin. *Mind and Matter.* Cambridge: Cambridge University Press, 1958.

100. Searles, Harold F. "The Effort to Drive the Other Person Crazy—An Element in the Aetiology and Psychotherapy of Schizophrenia." *British Journal of Medical Psychology* 32 (1959): 1–18, part 1.

101. Sechehaye, Marguerite. *Symbolic Realization.* New York: International University Press, 1951.

102. Selvini Palazzoli, Mara. *Self-Starvation: From the Intrapsychic to the Transpersonal Approach to Anorexia Nervosa.* London: Human Context Books, Chaucer Publishing Co., 1974.

103. ———, et al. "The Treatment of Children through Brief Therapy of Their Parents." *Family Process* 13 (1974): pp. 429–42.

104. Simonton, O. Carl, and Simonton, Stephanie. "Belief Systems and Management of the Emotional Aspects of Malignancy." *Journal of Transpersonal Psychology* 1 (1975): 29–47. Contains an extensive bibliography.

105. Sluzki, Carlos E., and Ransom, Donald C. *Double Bind. The Foundation of the Communicational Approach to the Family.* New York: Grune & Stratton, 1976.

106. Smith, Aaron. "Speech and Other Functions after Left (Dominant) Hemispherectomy." *Journal of Neurology, Neurosurgery, and Psychiatry* 29 (1966): 467–71.

107. Sperry, Roger W. "Hemispheric Deconnection and Unity in Conscious Awareness." *American Psychologist* 23 (1968): 723–33.

108. Spitz, René A. "Hospitalism." In *The Psychoanalytic Study of the Child.* vol. 1. New York: International University Press, 1945, pp. 53–74.

109. Spitzer, Daniel. *Wiener Spaziergänge* [Viennese Walks]. Munich: G. Müller, 1912, vol. 2., p. 42.

110. Starobinski, Jean. *La relation critique* [The Critical Relation]. Paris: Gallimard, 1970.

111. Varela G., Francisco J. "A Calculus for Self-Reference." *International Journal of General Systems* 2 (1975): 5–24. Introduced by Richard H. Howe and Heinz von Foerster. Ibid. 2 (1975): 1–3.

112. Verón, Eliseo. *Conducta, estructura y comunicación* [Behavior, Structure and Communication]. Buenos Aires: Editorial Jorge Alvarez, 1968, pp. 178–81.

113. Viehweg, Theodor. *Topik und Jurisprudenz* [Topic and Jurisprudence]. Munich: C. H. Beck, 1953, p. 22.

114. Wada, Juhn A. As quoted in *Science News* 110 (October 30, 1976): 277.

115. Watzlawick, Paul. *How Real Is Real? Confusion, Disinformation, Communication.* New York: Random House, 1976.

116. ———; Beavin, Janet H.; and Jackson, Don D. *Pragmatics of Human Communication: A Study of Interactional Patterns, Pathologies and Paradoxes.* New York: W. W. Norton, 1967.

117. ———; Weakland, John H.; and Fisch, Richard. *Change. Principles of Problem Formation and Problem Resolution.* New York: W. W. Norton, 1974.

118. Weakland, John H., and Jackson, Don D. "Patient and Therapist Observations on the Circumstances of a Schizophrenic Episode." *Archives of Neurology and Psychiatry* 79 (1958): 554–74.

119. Weder, Heinz. *Der Makler* [The Broker]. Bern: Kandelaber, 1969.

120. Wigan, Arthur L. *A New View of Insanity. The Duality of the Mind.* London: Longman, 1844. As quoted by Bogen (15, pp. 113–14).

121. Wittgenstein, Ludwig. *Remarks on the Foundations of Mathematics.* Oxford: Basil Blackwell, 1956, p. 100.

122. Wolfe, Tom. "The Me Decade and the Third Great Awakening." *New West,* August 1976, p. 35.

123. Xenophon. *Memorabilia IV,* 6:15.

124. Zangwil, Oliver L. "Speech and the Minor Hemisphere." *Acta Neurologica et Psychiatrica Belgica* 67 (1967): 1013–20.

INDEX

Act of Creation, The, 18, 55
Adler, Alfred, 42n
advertising, 11n, 65, 81–83
alcoholism, 87, 110
allusions, 78–90
ambiguity, 24, 78–90, 116
Anaximenes of Lampsacus, 7n
Antiphon of Athens, 7–8
antithetical sense of primary words, 24
aphorism, 69, 73–77
Aristotle, 7, 41n, 57n, 99, 108, 141, 150, 151
Arnim, Bettina von, 57n
asymmetry, cerebral, 19–39
Autogenic Training, 61, 63n
avoidance, 104n

Bakan, Paul, 36n, 56n
Bandler, Richard, and Grinder, John, 49n, 58n, 84, 104, 140
Bateson, Gregory, 36, 42n, 99
Bausani, Alessandro, 63–64
behavior prescriptions, 100, 127–37
Berger, Peter L., and Luckman, Thomas, 42n
Berlucchi, Carlo, 36n
Bettelheim, Bruno, 57n

body language, 9, 37
Bogen, Joseph E., 56n
brain research, 19–39; *see also* hemispheres, cerebral
Breton, André, 39n
Brown, George Spencer, 99n, 130
Buddhism, 41, 70, 96
Bukowski, Charles, 71n
Buñuel, Luis, 58

"Calculus for Self-Reference, A," 99n
cancer, 44, 61–62, 84
Canterbury Tales, 117n
caricature 23, 69
Castañeda, Carlos, 57n, 101
catharsis, 8
Charcot, Jean M., 39n
Chaucer, Geoffrey, 117n
chiasm, 74–77, 109
childhood memories, 34n
Chuang Tzu, 65
Cicero, 54
Cocteau, Jean, 26
commissurotomy, 20, 28–37, 56n; functional, 36, 91
communication: analogic, 15, 37, 47; digital, 15, 47, 53n; intraorganis-

communication (*continued*)
  mics, 4*n*; left-hemispheric, 21, 53,
  87; nonverbal, 9; pragmatics of, 6,
  8, 37–38; right-hemispheric, 24,
  46–47, 48–90
Communist Manifesto, 74
concretization, 68
condensation, 15, 24, 49–56
Condillac, Étienne de, 129
confusion technique, 93–95
consciousness industry, 11
corpus callosum, 20, 28–29, 36
culture, American, 10*n*
cybernetics, 42*n*, 99*n*

Dalí, Salvador, 39*n*
Darboux, Gaston, 16
Darwin, Charles, 34
Decline of the West, The, 52
deliberation, 41*n*
Demian, 155
denial, 104–05
depression, 43*n*, 100, 120–21, 143–44
depth psychology, 46, 73, 119
Dewson, James H., 21*n*
dialectics, 41*n*, 112*n*
Difficult Man, The, 88–89
Dimond, Stuart, 27
Direct Analysis, 57*n*
*Discreet Charm of the Bourgeoisie,
  The*, 58
dissociation theory, 36, 38, 103*n*
Doctor and the Soul, The, 120
Domenici, Gaston, 49–50
Domhoff, G. William, 35*n*
double bind, 99–100, 105, 114;
  pathogenic, 36–37, 105, 157;
  therapeutic, 105, 124, 160

Double Brain, The, 27
dream, 36*n*, 39*n*, 51, 56–58, 63, 96;
  and commissurotomy, 56*n*

Einstein, Albert, 46*n*, 128
Enzensberger, Hans M., 10
Epictetus, 42
epilepsy, 20*n*
Erickson, Milton H., 49, 57*n*, 58–63
  passim, 79, 84–85, 93–95, 106–07,
  113–15, 125–26, 132–35, 137,
  141–44, 146–48
Esterson, Aaron, 113*n*
euphemism, 80–81
Evans, J. Martin, 10*n*

faces, perception of, 22, 23
Fackel, Die, 51–52, 68
fairy tales, 51, 57*n*
Farb, Peter, 50–51
Finnegans Wake, 53
Fire Raisers, The, 43, 46
Fisch, Richard, 125
Foerster, Heinz von, 42*n*, 45, 130
Frankl, Viktor E., 55*n*, 101, 120
Frederick the Great, 79*n*
Frederick II, 5
Freud, Sigmund, 24, 39, 45*n*, 51, 55,
  76
frigidity, 62, 154
Frisch, Max, 43
Fry, William F., 55

Galin, David, 30, 33, 34, 35, 131
game without end, 126, 133

Index

Gauger, Hans-Martin, 79n
Gauss, Carl F., 16, 33
Gazzaniga, Michael S., 32, 33
Geschwind, Norman, 28–29
Gestalt therapy, 10, 57n
Giono, Jean, 50
Goethes Briefwechsel mit einem Kinde, 57n
Gombrich, Ernst H., 70
Gombrich, Richard, 70
Gordian knot, 118
Gordon, Harold W., 31
Gorgias, 8, 9
Grundgesetze des Sollens, 129

handedness, 21, 29–30
Hauser, Kaspar, 5n
Heine, Heinrich, 63n
Heisenberg, Werner, 128
hemispheres, cerebral, 19–39; integration of, 31, 32–9, 93; left: blocking of, 79, 84, 88, 91–126, 151; disturbances of, 22; functions of, 21, 46, 103; language of, 21, 53, 87; right: and arithmetic, 24–25; disturbances of, 26; functions of, 22–27, 46, 56, 61, 79; language of, 24, 46–47, 48–90; time perception of, 24, 93; and world image, 25, 128
hemispherectomy, 21
Hesse, Hermann, 56, 155
Hofmannsthal, Hugo von, 88
Hölderlin, Johann C. F., 74
holography, 22
Holton, Gerald, 46n
homonym, 78–79
homophony, 79, 87–88
Hoppe, Klaus, 36

hospitalism, 5
Hunter, John, 101
Huxley, Aldous, 92
hypnosis, hypnotherapy, 49, 51, 57–61, 66–67, 73, 79, 93–5, 97–8, 106, 116–17, 140; *see also* technique
Hypnotic Realities, 49

illusion of alternatives, 108–17, 119–20
Imperial Message, The, 13–14
injunction, injunctive language, 127–37
insomnia, 95–96, 100
Institutio Oratoria, 9
interspersal technique, 60–61, 84

Janet, Pierre, 36, 38, 39n, 103n
Jaspers, Karl, 25, 42, 44
Jaynes, Julian, 129
Jespèrsen, Otto, 5n
joke, 15, 54–56, 86; jokes and their relation to the unconscious, 54
Joyce, James, 53–54
"Judo"-technique, 144
Jung, Carl G., 16, 155

Kafka, Franz, 13
Kekulé, August, 18
Kelly, George A., 42n
Kennedy, Grace and Virginia, 6n

Kimura, Doreen, 31
koan, 96
Koestler, Arthur, 18, 54
Kopperschmidt, Josef, 6n, 41n, 74
Kraus, Karl, 51–52, 68
Kuhn, Thomas S., 18

Laing, Ronald D., 109, 113n
language, language forms, 13–18, 25,
    29, 32, 35, 46, 140; analogic, 15,
    37, 47; artificial, 6n, 64, 141; aver-
    sive, 67–68; body, 9, 37; concrete,
    68; development, 21n; digital, 15,
    47; figurative, 56–68; injunctive,
    127–37; left-hemispheric, 21, 53,
    87; patient's, use of, 139–44; posi-
    tive, 67–68; right-hemispheric 24,
    46–47, 48–90
Laws of Form, 99n, 130–31
Levy, Jerre, 23n
Liébeault, Ambroise A., 39n
life-threatening situations, 91–93
Logic of Commands, The, 130

MacKay, Donald, 32
magic formula, 65
Maillart, Robert, 17n
Make'em Laugh, 55
Mally, Ernst, 129
manipulation, 10–11
Mann, Thomas, 97
Mario and the Magician, 97–98
Marx, Karl, 42n, 112
mathematics, 17
Mauthe, Jörg, 54

Mesmer, Franz A., 39n
metaphor, 15, 54, 65, 78
"more of the same," 119, 145
Muir, Kenneth, 89
music, 22, 25–26, 35, 63n, 131
mysticism, 17, 96
mystification, 112

National Rifle Association, 76
Neanderthaler, 129
negation, 66
Nichomachean Ethics, 41n
Nietzsche, Friedrich, 43

obesity, 61, 87–88
olfaction, 22–23, 26, 31
oncology, 44, 61–62
onomatopoetic words, 16

Packard, Vance, 81
pain, pain control, 84, 95n, 106
paradox, 97, 99–100, 150; "be spon-
    taneous!" 100, 103, 122; counter-,
    110n; of self-reflexiveness, 44, 46,
    96
pars-pro-toto, 15, 16, 23, 26, 69–73
Pascal, Blaise, 117n
perception: acoustic, 31, 63n; body-,
    60; of faces, 22, 23, 26; of figures,
    25, 26, 93; music-, 22, 25–26, 35;
    number-, 21, 24–25, 29; object-,
    29–30; olfactory, 22–23, 26, 31;
    pain, 106; proprioceptive, 60; spa-

Index

tial, 25, 26; time-, 24, 93; visual, 30–31

Perls, Fritz, 10

Phantom of Liberty, The, 58

phobia, 137

Piaget, Jean, 42*n*

Pierce, John R., 24*n*

Plato, 8, 9, 26, 35*n*

Plaut, A., 155

pleroma, 46

Plutarch, 8

Poetics, 57*n*

poetry, 6*n*, 63–65

Poincaré, Henri, 16, 130

Popper, Karl R., 117

pragmatics (of communication), 6, 8, 37–38

preempting, 150–52

premises, search for, 42*n*

primary processes, 24, 91

primary words, antithetical meaning of, 24

pronuntiatio, 9

psychoanalysis, 21, 24, 38*n*, 53

psychodrama, 57*n*

psychosomatics, 36

psychosynthesis, 57*n*

psychotherapy, 36, 38, 46, 60; family, 38*n*, 109, 145, 157; hypno-, *see* hypnosis; marital, 132–35

pun, 15, 24, 78–90

Quintilian, 8–9

reality: adaptation, 12, 92; creation of, 16; first-order, 42, 76, 154; images of, 119; "objective," 42, 45; perception, *x*, 16, 23, 34, 46; second-order, 42, 43*n*, 76, 119, 154; *see also* world image

reframing, 8, 73, 118–27, 145

relation critique, La, 39*n*

remnant, unresolved, 67, 73, 107, 137

repression, 17, 31, 37

Republic, The, 35*n*

Rescher, Nicholas, 130

resistance, 139, 144–53; provocation of, 124, 145–6; use of, 144–50

resolution by motivation, 34

resolution by speed, 33

rhetoric: antique, 6–10; definition of, 6*n*; somatic, 9

Rhetorica ad Alexandrum, 7, 150–51

rhyme, *see* poetry

ritual, 154–56

Roda, Roda, 67

Rorschach test, 21, 24

Rosen, John N., 57*n*, 156

Rossi, Ernest L., 152

Salimbene of Parma, 5

Schill, Ferdinand, 75

schizophrenia, 24, 54, 108, 109, 112

Schmidt, Arno, 53

Schneider, Wolf, 16*n*, 42*n*, 83*n*

Schopenhauer, Arthur, 63

Schrödinger, Erwin, 44–45

Schwandbach bridge, 17*n*

Searles, Harold F., 110

Sechehaye, Marguerite, 156

secondary processes, 21

Selvini Palazzoli, Mara, 85, 156

Shakespeare, William, 78, 89

"sheep counting," 96

Simonton, O. Carl, 62

171

Sipos, Gyula, 74
Socrates, 7, 141
solution, wrong, as the problem, 102, 104*n*, 139, 146, 159
sophistry, 6–10
spatial perception, 25, 26
Spengler, Oswald, 52
Sperry, Roger W., 30–32
Spitz, René, 5
Spitzer, Daniel, 76
Starobinski, Jean, 39*n*, 47*n*
Steppenwolf, 56
Strauss, Richard, 26*n*
Structure of Magic, The, 58*n*
study problems, 121–24
surrealism, 39*n*
Sweet Madness, 55
symptom: displacement, 106; prescription, 101–05, 107
synonym, 79–81

Talleyrand, Périgod de, 69
technique: confusion, 88, 93–95; interspersal, 60–61, 84; "Judo"-, 144; ritual, 154–56; shingles, 153, "worst fantasy," 104
Tertullian, 84*n*
Tesla, Nikola, 18*n*
theory: mathematical, group, 99*n*; dissociation, 36, 38, 103*n*
thinking, thought, 15
thumb sucking, 121
Topica, 41*n*, 42*n*, 141
"Toward a Theory of Schizophrenia," 36, 99
trance, trance induction, 58–61, 93–95, 114–15, 153
Treatise on the Venereal Disease, A, 101–02
Two Gentlemen of Verona, The, 78

Ulysses, 53–56
Uses of Enchantment, The, 57*n*
utopia, utopian goals, 10, 12, 72, 73, 159

Varela, Francisco J., 99*n*
Verón, Eliseo, 81–83
Viehweg, Theodor, 42*n*, 141
Voltaire, François M., 79*n*

warts, 3
washing compulsion, 137
Weakland, John H., and Jackson, Don D., 108
Wechsler, Magi, 53
Weder, Heinz, 58–9
Wiener Spaziergänge, 76
Wigan, Arthur L., 19–20
Wilde, Oscar, 76
Wittgenstein, 124
world image, 12, 16, 25, 40–47, 57, 73, 93, 96, 132, 140, 144; and right hemisphere, 25, 128
"worst fantasy," 104

Xenophon, 141

Yoga, 31*n*

Zen, 56, 96
Zweig, Stefan, 39*n*